TIGER

**Center Point
Large Print**

**This Large Print Book carries the
Seal of Approval of N.A.V.H.**

TIGER

The Real Story

STEVE HELLING

CENTER POINT PUBLISHING
THORNDIKE, MAINE

This Center Point Large Print edition
is published in the year 2010 by arrangement with
Da Capo Press, a member of the Perseus Books Group.

The text of this Large Print edition is unabridged.
In other aspects, this book may vary
from the original edition.
Printed in the United States of America
on permanent paper.
Set in 16-point Times New Roman type.

ISBN: 978-1-60285-841-1

Library of Congress Cataloging-in-Publication Data

Helling, Steve.
  Tiger : the real story / Steve Helling. — Large print ed.
      p. cm.
  Originally published: New York : DaCapo Press, 2010.
  ISBN 978-1-60285-841-1 (library binding : alk. paper)
  1. Woods, Tiger. 2. Golfers—United States—Biography. 3. Large type books. I. Title.
  GV964.W66H45 2010
  796.352092—dc22
  [B]

                                                        2010012853

FOR MY WIFE, EMMA,
WITH LOVE

CONTENTS

PROLOGUE

I FIRST MET TIGER WOODS on October 6, 2002. It was a sunny Sunday morning at his home course of Isleworth, Florida, and Tiger was playing best-ball scramble with four average Joes who had won a sweepstakes with Upper Deck sports cards. I was invited to ride along with Tiger for the first nine holes and ask him a few questions. Nothing too personal, his agent had warned me. Questions about his new girlfriend, Elin Nordegren, would get me tossed off the property within seconds.

I had met his father, Earl, the previous June during the Tiger Woods Junior Golf Clinic at Walt Disney World. He had talked for nearly an hour, repeating amusing, candid, and downright embarrassing anecdotes from Tiger's youth. Earl was a master of oversharing, and Tiger had learned to smile in an aw-shucks way at his father's long-winded stories. If Tiger was annoyed by his father's bravado, he didn't show it.

Earl may have been an interviewer's dream, but Tiger had a reputation of being a Cheshire cat, known to grin and disappear when asked questions he didn't want to answer. Tiger's team members made clear to me that he could end the interview at any time, and they recommended that I not ask anything offensive.

I met Tiger on the golf course, and he gave me a

polite, yet firm handshake as we climbed into his cart. It was a shallow conversation, the equivalent of elevator small talk. We chatted about baseball cards, hip-hop artists, and sports drinks. We shared workout tips. I admired his pimped-out golf cart, complete with neon running lights and a six-speaker sound system. What I learned about Tiger that day: He loved *Caddyshack* but hated *Caddyshack II.* He was self-conscious about his skinny calves. He liked to ski. He loved pink lemonade. He sweated a lot while golfing in the oppressive Florida heat and humidity, so he had a half-dozen extra shirts in his golf cart.

We didn't talk much about golf that day; his one-stroke loss at the 2002 PGA Tournament was still painfully fresh in his mind, and he was teetering on the edge of a slump that would last nearly three years. Still, Tiger was engaging, relaxed, and occasionally funny as we developed a rapport that made him an easy interview. I liked him immediately.

On April 16, 2004, I met Tiger again, this time at Fort Bragg, North Carolina. Tiger had spent the previous week running obstacle courses, shooting rifles, and polishing boots with the Green Berets. Earl Woods had been assigned to a Special Forces unit at Fort Bragg in 1967, and Tiger wanted to take a training tour to honor his father.

The military week had made Tiger a little more introspective than he had been at our last meeting; wearing his camouflage uniform with his name above the left pocket, Tiger was willing to open up a little bit more. "I've always taken the creed that you can be young once, but immature forever," he said. "I think I'm growing up now."

Tiger was in midslump by then—he had finished twenty-second in the 2004 Masters five days earlier —and he was in a reflective mood, like a teenager leaving summer camp for the cold reality of the next school year. He looked longingly at the waiting Humvee and sighed. "If I weren't a golfer," he said, "I would have trained for Special Ops."

I was on hand for his October 5, 2004, wedding. Wearing a tan suit and white shirt, a serene Tiger stood on a Barbados hillside and pledged to spend his life with Elin Nordegren for better or worse, richer or poorer, in sickness and in health. As Tiger's face was illuminated by a spectacular fireworks display at the reception, the optimism in his eyes was unmistakable. Whatever would happen later, he seemed to believe on that picturesque evening that this was a permanent union, and he was ready to share his amazing life with his stunning new wife.

The next time I sat down with him was on January 26, 2005. Married for less than four months, the newlywed Tiger exuded an optimistic glow as we chatted about his marriage, his dreams for the future, and his desire for children. His professional resurgence had just begun, including a win at the Buick Invitational just three days earlier. He had regained his confidence on the course and would go on to win the Masters that year. It was the most candid Tiger would ever be with me, and he talked openly about his new bride. "I knew that Elin was a special woman pretty soon after I met her," he enthused with pride. "I knew that she was the one for me. She's a special person, and I know how lucky I am to have her. We're at the beginning of our life together, and that's an exciting place to be."

The excitement of Elin was still new, and Tiger beamed as he talked about her. It wasn't a grin or a sly smile; it was a wide-eyed, open-mouthed exuberance that can come only from personal fulfillment and happiness. "I married Elin because I see a long future with her," he boldly declared.

I spent several hours with Tiger that day, watching him put on a reflective suit to do a motion capture session for his video game *Tiger Woods PGA Tour 2006*. He had famously modified his swing, and he wanted to update the video game to reflect his real-life changes. He was in a good mood, and the conversation flowed easily. I had recently covered the divorce of Brad Pitt and Jennifer Aniston, and Tiger was surprisingly interested in knowing the details. He wondered aloud if Angelina Jolie was really the "other woman." He asked me about Nicole Kidman and Tom Cruise. It was a human conversation that was shockingly commonplace; it was surprising that Tiger Woods—one of the world's biggest and most private stars—cared about the lives of other celebrities whom he had never met.

But that was the paradox of Tiger Woods. The more I talked to him, the less I knew about him. Every answer he gave would raise ten more queries, but his limited time made it impossible for me to ask enough follow-up questions.

The last time I spoke to Tiger, on June 25, 2009, the carefree exuberance had been replaced by a weary worldliness. He had spent a frenetic morning promoting his video game in Times Square, but he was more than physically drained; he seemed emotionally fatigued. As I sat down with him, the conversation drifted to his father, who had died three years earlier. "My dad passed away before Sam [Tiger's daughter] was born," he said evenly, "so I didn't have a chance to talk to him about being a father. I regret that. I will always regret that."

Father's Day had just passed; it was the first one since the birth of his son, Charlie Axel. Tiger didn't celebrate with his family; he was busy playing in the U.S. Open. But he acknowledged that his memories of Earl Woods made it a hard day for him. "I think of him every day," he told me. "He taught me everything. I hear his voice."

Tiger got a faraway look in his eye as he told me the oft-repeated story of his father teaching him to play golf: the white high chair in the garage, Earl practicing his swing, Tiger's fascination with the sport. The coaching, the mind games, the training. It was almost as if Tiger believed that talking about Earl's influence would keep him alive, at least for the moment.

Over the years, I had heard rumors of Tiger's partying—drunken nights at the clubs, dirty dancing with other women, phone numbers slipped to pretty blondes—but I didn't follow up on the tips. For one thing, the stories were nearly impossible to verify, and the sources were usually questionable characters: strip club bouncers, self-promoting club owners, and tabloid reporters. But my unwillingness to follow up on the tips was also self-preservation. Negative coverage of Tiger—or even positive coverage that wasn't approved and micromanaged—would often result in swift, permanent excommunication from the Tiger Woods camp. It was in everyone's best interest to sweep the rumors under the rug.

Through hours of interviews, press conferences, red carpets, and events, Tiger Woods seldom spoke a single word to me that he didn't intend to say. Sometimes candid and sometimes elusive—his manner really depended on his mood—Tiger was his own gatekeeper, painstakingly building his persona with each carefully crafted sentence. It took thirteen calculated years to meticulously shape his image. It took two weeks to destroy it.

CHAPTER 1

ON THE NIGHT that everything fell apart, November 27, 2009, Tiger Woods ran barefoot out of his mansion, shivering as he fled into the cold November air. Wearing nothing but khaki shorts and a dark blue T-shirt, he clambered into the driver's seat of his black Cadillac Escalade. As the brand-new vehicle sped out of his driveway, its screeching tires left telltale black skid marks on the stone-colored driveway. Tiger quickly lost control of the Escalade; within fifty yards of his front door, the vehicle careened into a row of hedges, drove over a curb, and swerved into a fire hydrant before ultimately plowing into a neighbor's oak tree at thirty miles per hour. Seconds later, illuminated by the lights from nearby homes and the one remaining working headlight on the Escalade, the world's most recognizable athlete lay amid the shattered glass on the street, unconscious and bleeding from the mouth. His gorgeous blonde wife, Elin, knelt by his side, cradling his head against her black jogging suit. Two golf clubs—a wedge and a bent nine iron— lay on the ground next to her. The disabled Escalade's engine sputtered and knocked loudly, nearly drowning out the sound of Elin's sobs.

It would have been a dramatic scene anywhere, but it was especially jarring to neighbors accustomed to the calm serenity of Isleworth, a premier golfing community where the rows of multimillion-dollar mansions sat staidly next to a lush golf course. Isleworth was a cocoon of exclusivity, insulating its wealthy residents from dramatic incidents such as this. The neighborhood was a beautiful fortress, gated and safe, with a security team patrolling the streets in marked cars. Even police officers from the nearby town of Windermere were required to ask for permission to enter the gates of Isleworth, although the need arose very infrequently.

In the mansion next door, Kimberly Harris awoke with a start. Lying quietly in bed, she listened to the steady knocking of the Escalade's dying engine and tried to make sense of what she was hearing. At first, she wondered if someone was banging on the front door; perhaps her brother had forgotten his keys and was locked outside. She slipped out of bed, careful not to awaken the young niece who was sleeping next to her. Quietly descending the grand staircase of the home, she checked all the downstairs bedrooms. All were sleeping soundly in their beds, unaware of the bizarre scene unfolding just a few dozen feet from where they slept. Kimberly peered out the window and saw an unfamiliar black SUV at the base of the driveway, its lone headlight shining directly into her house.

She softly knocked on the bedroom door of her brother, twenty-seven-year-old Jairus Adams.

Receiving no response, she knocked louder and harder until he finally woke out of his deep sleep. She quickly explained what she had seen. "I don't know who's outside, but I think you need to go out there and find out what's happening," she said, "but please be careful."

Jairus left the warmth of the mansion, bracing himself against the chill of the autumn air. As he trudged down the driveway toward the disabled vehicle, the night's stillness was palpable: Another benefit to living in Isleworth was the community's commitment to quiet. The silence framed the sound of Elin's sniffling and another, more surprising sound: Tiger Woods snoring as if he had simply fallen asleep in the middle of the street. It was clear to Jairus that Tiger, lying perpendicular to the Escalade, had been pulled out of the vehicle and onto the pavement. Jairus crouched down and looked at his famous neighbor; his lips were cut and bleeding, and his teeth were stained blood red. Jairus smelled no alcohol on the golfer's breath.

Elin hovered over her husband, gently shaking his shoulders and trying to wake him up. "Tiger," she whispered plaintively. "Tiger, are you okay?" Upon receiving no response, she raised her voice, becoming more urgent. "Tiger," she said sharply, "Tiger, can you hear me?"

If Tiger could hear her, he didn't answer. He continued to snore, never opening his eyes or acknowledging the growing panic in his young wife's voice. Elin turned to Jairus. "Please help me," she begged, her pretty face twisted with fear. "Can you please help me? I don't have a phone with me. Will you call someone?"

Jairus sprinted back to the house to call for help. As he entered the front door, he called to his sister. "Bring some blankets and pillows outside," he said. "Tiger is down." He then picked up the house phone and dialed 911, being careful not to mention Tiger Woods by name.

Partway through the call, Tiger's mother, Kultida, sprinted out of the Woods family home. She assessed the scene instantly and turned to Jairus, her face twisted into a question mark of concern. "What happened?"

"We're trying to figure [that] out right now," Jairus responded. "We're just trying to get the police here right now. We don't know what happened. We're figuring that out right now. I'm on the phone with the police right now."

Kultida Woods stepped over to Elin and whispered into her ear; both women looked at Tiger again as Kultida wiped her eyes.

Dispatcher 1: 911 what's your emergency?
Jairus Adams: I need an ambulance immediately. I have someone down in front of my house. They hit a pole. I came out to see.
Dispatcher 1: Sir, is it a car accident? Hello? Sir? Hello?

Jairus Adams: Hello, yes.

Dispatcher 1: Now are they trapped inside of the vehicle?

Jairus Adams: No, they're laying on the ground now.

Dispatcher 1: OK, sir, medical is on the line sir, OK?

Dispatcher 2: Fire-rescue. What happened? What's wrong?

Jairus Adams: I have a neighbor, he hit the tree. And we came out here just to see what was going on. I see him and he's laying down.

Dispatcher 2: OK, are you able to tell if he's breathing?

Jairus Adams: No, I can't tell right now.

Dispatcher 2: OK. We do have help on the way. What color is his car, too?

Jairus Adams: It's a black Escalade.

(Background, Kultida Woods yelling): WHAT HAPPENED?

Jairus Adams (to Kultida): We're trying to figure [that] out right now. We're just trying to get the police here right now. We don't know what happened. We're figuring that out right now. I'm on the phone with the police right now.

Dispatcher 2: OK. We got paramedics on the way.

Jairus Adams: OK, OK, thank you.

It had been a slow night for the Windermere Police Department, which wasn't unusual for the

19

small precinct of only thirteen officers. Since nightfall, they had responded to four calls: a domestic incident, two minor traffic accidents, and a panicked old woman who had eaten too much Thanksgiving turkey and mistaken her heartburn for cardiac arrest. Windermere just wasn't a place where very much happened, and that's what its residents wanted. In this town located just eight miles outside the Orlando city limits, the average homeowner was a respectable, productive member of society who had paid more than $800,000 for a Spanish-style home. People moved into Windermere to escape crimes, not commit them. The resulting low crime rate gave the police force a lot of downtime.

The crown jewel of Windermere was the Isleworth subdivision, where the average house cost more than $4 million. In addition to Tiger Woods, other notables called Isleworth home: NBA stars Shaquille O'Neal and Grant Hill owned mansions there. Actor Wesley Snipes had recently moved out. Business leaders and society members lived their lives of luxury within the gates, and they very seldom needed to call the police.

Officers Jason Sipos and Brandon McDonnell were conducting their routine patrol when they received a call to respond to an accident at 6432 Deacon Circle. Although they instantly recognized that the address was inside the gates of

Isleworth, they didn't immediately make the connection with the golfing superstar. Turning on the cruiser's siren and blue lights, they sped toward the scene, momentarily pausing at the Isleworth gates to get permission from the security guard to enter the neighborhood. The car stopped at the scene, its blue lights reflecting off the shiny Escalade. Tiger was still unconscious, covered by a red blanket with a pillow tucked under his neck. Assessing the situation, the officers knelt down on the pavement next to him. Officer Sipos held the golfer's head and neck steady while Officer McDonnell, a former paramedic, checked Tiger's vital signs and began to administer first aid.

Tiger moaned loudly and stirred. He opened his eyes, looking straight ahead, yet did not focus on anything. He tried to move, but his efforts were thwarted by a combination of the officers holding him down and his own inability to control his body. His eyes suddenly rolled back into his head, and he lost consciousness again. Fearing that he had suffered a spinal injury, McDonnell and Sipos continued to restrain Tiger while waiting for the paramedics. The golfer began to shiver uncontrollably in the forty-degree chill; a cough turned into a sputter, and tiny droplets of blood sprayed into the air.

Within minutes, an ambulance arrived, its red lights combining with the police cruiser's blue flashers to illuminate the entire street. A growing gaggle of onlookers sleepily emerged from their homes, partly to see if they could help and partly to gawk at the unfolding scene.

As paramedics jumped out of the ambulance, one of them draped his arm around Elin and gently led her away from Tiger. She started protesting loudly. "That's my husband," she shrieked loudly. "You can't keep me away from him. Let me be with him." The paramedics tried to calm her, but Elin's concern became more hysterical as she called out to her fallen husband.

Ignoring her repeated pleas, paramedics quickly assessed Tiger's vital signs. His blood pressure was steady; his pulse was strong. Although he was bleeding from the mouth, there was no additional sign of trauma to his head. They exchanged worried glances with the police officers; there were very few external injuries, yet Tiger had been unconscious for nearly ten minutes. He was either impaired, or he had suffered a brain injury. They just couldn't tell yet.

Paramedics began testing for paralysis by applying painful stimuli to his left foot. Tiger groaned as he opened his eyes again, and his pupils rolled back into his head while his eyelids stayed open, causing the onlookers to gasp at the whites of his eyes. Neighbors would later describe his eyes as looking "lifeless and dead." One of Isleworth's security guards, stunned at the disturbing scene, began to recite the Lord's

Prayer. Elin, her tear-stained face illuminated by the ambulance lights, started to shriek. Kultida put her arm around Elin for comfort, and the two women huddled together in the cold.

A paramedic pulled Elin aside and quietly asked her if Tiger was on any medication; she responded that she knew he took medication but didn't know what kind. She dashed toward the house with a police officer at her heels. When she got to the front door, she turned to the officer. "Wait here, please," she said to him as she slipped into the foyer. The officer tried to look past her into the home, but he saw nothing before she quickly closed the door. Minutes later, she emerged from the home with two brown pill bottles of prescription medication. One of them contained the sedative Ambien, a sleep aid with a relatively low potential for abuse. The second bottle contained Vicodin, a physically and psychologically addictive narcotic analgesic used for pain management. The paramedic put the bottles in a plastic bag to transport them to the hospital along with the golfer. If Tiger were under the influence of these drugs, his driving would certainly be compromised.

A black-and-tan police cruiser from the Florida Highway Patrol pulled up to the scene, its flashing lights adding to the chaos of the moment. Stepping out of the vehicle, Trooper Joshua Evans joined the conversation and asked Elin if Tiger had recently consumed any alcohol.

"Yes," Elin replied, "he drank some earlier tonight."

The officer made a note of it; if he suspected that Tiger was impaired, he wasn't saying anything. He called the Florida Highway Patrol dispatch.

After telling the operator that he was working the Tiger Woods accident, the dispatcher asked about Tiger's well-being. "Is he okay?"

"Yes," replied Evans. "He's got minor injuries."

The dispatcher chose her words carefully. "Was he, um, doing something he shouldn't have been doing to cause it?"

"No, um, he's—he's good," Evans answered.

"He's a good golf player, I know that," the dispatcher responded, as they both laughed.

"But not a good driver," Evans chuckled. "He's a little banged up, I guess. That's all."

"Yeah, probably a little confused," the dispatcher replied.

After he hung up the phone, Evans filled out accident report forms. The hospital would do a blood test, and he could subpoena the results.

As Officer Evans walked in a circle around the disabled Escalade, he noted the vehicle's damage on his crash report. Both front fenders were bent, and the front bumper dangled precariously from the damaged grill. Fluid dripped from underneath the engine, indicating damage to the engine block. He estimated the damage to be $8,000. He inspected the interior of the vehicle and saw a pair of sandals on the floor in front of the passenger seat. He noted that the airbags hadn't deployed, meaning that Tiger had to have been going less than thirty-three miles per hour. More confusing were the rear windows; they had both been smashed from the outside—damage that was inconsistent with the accident scene.

As paramedics lifted the golfer's gurney into the back of the ambulance to take him to the hospital, he opened his eyes once again, dazed at his surroundings. Elin looked at him and mouthed, "I love you." He opened his mouth to speak, but lost consciousness before he could answer.

TWELVE HOURS LATER, news of the crash still hadn't made the local papers, and Tiger's managers briefly hoped they'd be able to keep the entire incident under wraps. After all, Tiger had the reputation for being a private celebrity who chose not to offer his personal life for public consumption. The strategy of secrecy had been extremely successful, and Tiger's career had been scandal-free for more than thirteen years. Perhaps the event wouldn't garner many headlines over the long Thanksgiving weekend; most newspapers and magazines had only a skeleton crew working. Hopefully, they wouldn't notice. Maybe this would just go away.

November had started out well enough for Tiger when he eked out a two-shot victory at the Australian Masters, pocketing $3 million in the process. "I've never won down here, so now I have won on every continent, except for Antarctica," he bragged in a post-tournament press conference. "I haven't played the Antarctica Four-Ball yet. But to have won on every playable continent, it's something I've always wanted to do. And now I've done that."

But as the Thanksgiving holidays approached, rumors of his infidelity were gaining momentum and threatening to tarnish his squeaky-clean image. The week before the car crash, the *National Enquirer* had run an explosive story claiming that Tiger was having a sexual affair with a stunning Manhattan party planner, Rachel Uchitel. The story was explicit in its details, including an eye-witness account of Rachel meeting Tiger in his hotel room during the Australian Masters earlier in the month. Rachel's friends told the tabloid that Tiger and Rachel had sent each other dozens of sexually explicit text messages. The article even quoted Rachel as saying, "It's Tiger Woods! I don't care about his wife! We're in love."

Tiger's team hoped that these rumors would stay in the realm of the tabloids; as long as they never made it to the legitimate press, people wouldn't believe them. More importantly, team members hoped that the rumors wouldn't significantly damage Tiger's marketability; in addition to being a celebrity, he was a commodity. Any negative press could tarnish his brand, resulting in financial setbacks for everyone around him.

A few members of Tiger's team were secretly worried about the power of the *Enquirer:* In 2008, the tabloid had printed a devastating series of stories chronicling former presidential hopeful John Edwards's extramarital affair with a videographer, and the report had begun a domino effect that would eventually destroy the charismatic senator's reputation, along with any chances he'd ever have of higher office in the future. Tiger's team members hoped that wouldn't happen this time, especially if the rumors were true. It was best to maintain a "don't ask, don't tell" policy in Tiger's camp. If he really was having affairs, it was in his managers' best interest to intentionally keep themselves in the dark.

At 3:15 p.m. on Friday afternoon, however, any hope of keeping Tiger's story quiet were dashed. The *Orlando Sentinel* ran a short story on its Web site, reporting that Tiger Woods had been "seriously injured" in a one-car crash near his home and taken to Health Central Hospital in the nearby town of Ocoee. The story quoted a press release from Florida Highway Patrol spokeswoman Kim Montes. The statement would have been unremarkable except for nine words that would infuse it with an ominous sense of foreboding: "The crash remains under investigation and charges are pending."

The day after Thanksgiving is traditionally a slow news day, one of the slowest of the year, so editors were eager to run a story of the world's most famous athlete getting into a bizarre car crash. Within an hour, the shocking news was repeated on more than two hundred news Web sites around the globe. Bloggers speculated that Tiger must have been impaired to have had such a serious accident so late at night near his home. News vans parked outside the hospital, hoping for a shot of Tiger or Elin entering or leaving the hospital.

As it turned out, Tiger was not seriously injured; he was quickly treated for the cuts on his lips and released from the hospital on Saturday afternoon, smuggled out a side entrance into a waiting vehicle. By the time the media realized he had been discharged from the hospital, he was safely within the gates of Isleworth, protected from news cameras and inquisitive reporters.

The next wave of news hit the press on Saturday evening when the Windermere Police chief told news outlets that Elin claimed to have used two golf clubs to shatter the rear windows of the vehicle after the crash in an attempt to pull her injured husband to safety. Members of the media were skeptical; the story made little logistical sense. Why would she have two golf clubs handy? And why smash out both back windows?

By the morning of Saturday, November 28—less than thirty-six hours after the accident—the speculation had become deafening. TMZ.com, a celebrity gossip Web site with a successful history of breaking scandalous stories, reported that Tiger's injuries had been inflicted by Elin, not by the car accident. Citing an unnamed friend of Tiger's, the report claimed that Elin had confronted him about the *Enquirer* story that he was seeing another woman. The argument got heated, and, according to TMZ, Elin scratched Tiger's face. The source then told TMZ that Tiger quickly retreated to his SUV, only to have Elin follow after him with the golf clubs, which she used to strike the vehicle several times as he drove away. Whether this story was true or not wasn't important, at least not to the American people. It was a fascinating narrative, and most people believed it to be the closest approximation to the truth that anyone would learn.

In thirteen years of public prominence, Tiger Woods had never gotten any significant negative press. Sure, he had thrown temper tantrums on the golf course, and he was known to curse a blue streak—sometimes in earshot of the cameras. But Tiger's image was wholesome, and he had a reputation for being disciplined, even robotic. His inner circle had never had to deal with a real scandal; Tiger was just above it all. But now that a scandal was quickly unfolding, Tiger's team quickly met to decide the next course of action. Team members hastily penned a statement and posted it on Tiger's Web site:

As you all know, I had a single-car accident earlier this week, and sustained some injuries. I have some cuts, bruising and right now I'm pretty sore.

This situation is my fault, and it's obviously embarrassing to my family and me. I'm human and I'm not perfect. I will certainly make sure this doesn't happen again.

This is a private matter and I want to keep it that way. Although I understand there is curiosity, the many false, unfounded and malicious rumors that are currently circulating about my family and me are irresponsible.

The only person responsible for the accident is me. My wife, Elin, acted courageously when she saw I was hurt and in trouble. She was the first person to help me. Any other assertion is absolutely false.

This incident has been stressful and very difficult for Elin, our family and me. I appreciate all the concern and well wishes that we have received. But, I would also ask for some understanding that my family and I deserve some privacy no matter how intrusive some people can be.

Meanwhile, the Florida Highway Patrol continued to investigate the crash. Two troopers drove to Windermere to interview Tiger on Saturday afternoon, hoping that he would shed some light on the previous night's events. As they arrived at the front gates of Isleworth, one of the officer's cell phones rang. It was Tiger's agent, Mark Steinberg. "Tiger can't meet with you today. He's really not feeling well," Steinberg told the officer. "Can we do this tomorrow, instead?" The officers agreed and drove back to the station.

Tiger's unwillingness to meet with officers rankled the top brass at the Florida Highway Patrol, prompting spokeswoman Kim Montes to release a terse statement. "The Florida Highway Patrol has received information that Tiger Woods and his wife were not available to be interviewed by state troopers as we had previously scheduled. This announcement came from his agent. Troopers were asked to return tomorrow. This is an ongoing crash investigation."

The rescheduled interview with troopers was slated for 3:00 p.m. on Sunday, November 29. Paparazzi lined up by the gates of Isleworth in anticipation of the questioning, hoping to get a picture of the cops arriving, but the wait was in vain. Two hours before the scheduled interview, the Florida Highway Patrol received a phone call from Mark NeJame, a prominent Orlando attorney who had been retained by Tiger. The interview wasn't going to happen, at least not that day.

The Florida Highway Patrol issued another brusque statement. "Just after 1:00 p.m., lawyer Mark NeJame contacted the Florida Highway

Patrol to inform us that he is representing Tiger Woods. Mark NeJame stated that the interview that was scheduled for today has been canceled. The traffic crash remains under investigation and charges are pending."

The media latched onto the last three words of the press release. "Charges are pending." What did they mean?

Shortly after noon on Monday, November 30, the Florida Highway Patrol issued another press release, the latest in its transparent display of annoyance. "As of Nov. 30, 2009, the Florida Highway Patrol has been unable to speak to Mr. Woods about the crash he was involved in on the morning of Nov. 27, 2009, despite attempts to do so. Mr. Woods' representatives have provided us with his driver license information, vehicle registration and current proof of insurance, as required by Florida Law. The crash investigation is ongoing and charges are pending."

Tiger's Escalade was in police impound, where Corporal Tom Dewitt snapped dozens of pictures of the disabled vehicle. There were bottles of water, broken glass, and a thin paperback book called *Get a Grip on Physics,* certainly nothing to indicate any illegal activity. The windshield was still intact, and there was no sign of blood anywhere in the vehicle. Dewitt headed to Isleworth, where he took pictures of the accident scene. Thanks to Florida's liberal public records laws, the media quickly got the 105 photos and splashed the indelible images across newspaper front pages throughout the country.

That same day, Trooper Joshua Evans submitted a Request for Investigative Subpoena, asking for access to Tiger's blood results from Health Central Hospital. Although he had told the dispatcher that he didn't believe Tiger was impaired, something had clearly changed his opinion. In the narrative section of the request, Trooper Evans wrote: "The driver lost control of his vehicle, crashed and was transported to the hospital. A witness stated that the driver had consumed alcohol earlier in the day and the same witness removed the driver from the vehicle after the collision. Also, the same witness stated that the driver was prescribed medication (Ambien and Vicodin). Impairment of the driver is also suspected due to the careless driving that resulted in the traffic crash."

Less than an hour later, Trooper Evans received his answer: Assistant State Attorney Steve Foster, head of the State Attorney's Office's Intake Division, denied the request. At the bottom of the form, he scrawled, "Insufficient information provided to lawfully issue subpoena."

The refusal of the State Attorney's Office to issue the subpoena irritated many of the officers within the Florida Highway Patrol, who felt that they had sufficient evidence to warrant a subpoena. "I have gotten subpoenas issued with a lot less evidence than that," said one of the officers involved in the case. "I don't know why the sub-poena wasn't issued; I really don't. All I know is that everything was done by the book, and I believe that subpoena should have been issued."

Later that afternoon, another bombshell rocked Tiger: Jaimee Grubbs, a cocktail waitress from Los Angeles, went public with a voicemail that she claimed Tiger had left on her cell phone. "Hey, it's Tiger," he said furtively. "I need you to do me a huge favor. Can you please take your name off your phone? My wife went through my phone and may be calling you. So if you can, please take your name off that. Just have it as a number on the voicemail. You got to do this for me. Huge. Quickly. Bye." It was the first evidence of an inappropriate affair that any of Tiger's alleged women would have, and the voicemail found its way onto cable news stations that evening.

Grubbs then provided the media with more than three hundred text messages that she claimed to have received from Tiger. Some of the messages were mundane, whereas others took on a rabid—almost frantic—sexual tone. "I will wear you out soon," one message promised. "When was the last time you got laid?" Surprisingly, many of the mes-sages were more romantic than they were sexual. "Quiet and secretively we will always be together," he had predicted by text in September 2009. The romantic texts were more damaging than the sexual ones: This was not merely a hookup; it was a relationship. The most recent text message had been sent four days earlier, on Thanksgiving morning. "Happy thanksgiving to u," he had written at 11:15 in the morning. "U too love" she had replied.

The public frenzy was all over the airwaves and the Internet, but things were decidedly quieter inside the Woods home as Tiger and Elin began to work through their personal anguish. During a long conversation, Elin demanded answers. "I want to know what else to expect," she insisted of her husband. "Who else is going to come forward?"

As Tiger detailed his indiscretions, Elin grew more agitated. Anger and tears gave way to silence, and the couple's fragile relationship became suddenly distant, as if they were two strangers who happened to live in the same house. Tiger owned a second home in the neighborhood that had once belonged to his father, Earl Woods. He quietly moved some clothes into the second home and began to sleep there. Elin, still reeling from the injurious confessions, remained in the family home with the children.

On Tuesday, December 1, troopers were finally able to meet with Tiger Woods at his Isleworth home. Flanked by his attorney and his agent, Tiger politely answered the officers' questions and even lifted his shirt to show them his torso and abdomen. Officers observed that Tiger had a fat lip from the incident, but no other visible injuries. The officers determined that Tiger's injuries were consistent with an impact on the vehicle's steering wheel. They issued him a $164 ticket for careless driving, which he signed and paid during the meeting.

Three hours later, more than 100 reporters and cameramen packed a crowded room at the Florida Highway Patrol, and news of the careless driving charge was beamed around the world. Legally, the case of *Florida v. Tiger Woods* was closed.

But the public appetite had been whetted. By Wednesday, the story had spread like wildfire, attaining a level of notoriety usually reserved for the juiciest sex scandals. Tiger released another statement on his Web site:

I have let my family down and I regret those transgressions with all of my heart. I have not been true to my values and the behavior my family deserves. I am not without faults and I am far short of perfect. I am dealing with my behavior and personal failings behind closed doors with my family. Those feelings should be shared by us alone.

Although I am a well-known person and have made my career as a professional athlete, I have been dismayed to realize the full extent of what tabloid scrutiny really means. For the last week, my family and I have been hounded to expose intimate details of our personal lives. The stories in particular that physical violence played any role in the car accident were utterly false and malicious. Elin has always done more to support our family and shown more grace than anyone could possibly expect.

But no matter how intense curiosity about public figures can be, there is an important and deep principle at stake, which is the right to some simple, human measure of privacy. I realize there are some who don't share my view on that. But for me, the virtue of privacy is one that must be protected in matters that are intimate and within one's own family.

Personal sins should not require press releases and problems within a family shouldn't have to mean public confessions.

Whatever regrets I have about letting my family down have been shared with and felt by us alone. I have given this a lot of reflection and thought and I believe that there is a point at which I must stick to that principle even though it's difficult.

I will strive to be a better person and the husband and father that my family deserves. For all of those who have supported me over the years, I offer my profound apology.

But the scandal wasn't over yet. In fact, it was just beginning. The floodgates of women had already opened; one by one, they came forward, each with varying degrees of credibility and proof of her alleged affair with the golfer. They came forward with perverse new details that seemed to increase in salaciousness, as if each mistress wanted to outdo the woman who had come before.

The third alleged mistress emerged just hours after the statement went live on Tiger's Web site. Kalika Moquin, a twenty-seven-year-old marketing executive from Las Vegas, was linked to the golfer on the evening of December 2. Sources told a supermarket tabloid that the sexual affair had begun in mid-2007, and that Tiger had told Kalika that he was unhappy with the pressures of married life. Kalika refused to confirm or deny a relationship with the golfer, telling *Life & Style* magazine: "It's not appropriate for me to comment one way or the other. At this time, I'm just choosing to focus on my job."

Shortly after the emergence of Kalika, Tiger suffered a personal blow that hurt him greatly: A personal friend spoke out against him for the first time. Jesper Parnevik, the Swedish golfer who had introduced Tiger and Elin, came out swinging against him. "I really feel sorry for Elin," Parnevik told reporters at the PGA Tour's qualifying tournament in West Palm Beach. "Me and my wife were at fault for hooking her up with him. We probably thought he was a better guy than he is. I would probably need to apologize to her and hope she uses a driver next time instead of the 3-iron.

"It's a private thing of course," he continued. "But when you are the guy he is, the world's best athlete, you should think more before you do stuff, and maybe not just do it, like Nike says."

The same day, another bombshell exploded when TMZ reported that Tiger had not acted alone in his infidelity. TMZ's Web site alleged that Bryon Bell, Tiger's best friend from high school, had arranged for Rachel Uchitel to visit Tiger in Melbourne in November, setting up the tryst that would eventually destroy Tiger's image. The Web site released an e-mail from Bryon to Rachel dated November 9. "Here are the details for all the flights," the e-mail read. "Sorry for all the changes. I look forward to meeting you tomorrow. Bryon." Attached to the e-mail was an itinerary: Rachel would fly from New York to Australia and would stay at the Crown Towers Hotel in Melbourne—the same hotel where Tiger was staying as he played in the Australian Masters. What no one knew was that the *National Enquirer* was aware of the plan and sent a reporter to track them. After the reporter watched Rachel check into the hotel, the *Enquirer* editors decided they had enough material to run a story. Tiger was scheduled to be the best man at Bryon's wedding the following weekend; he never showed up.

On December 6, a fourth woman came forward. Mindy Lawton was a thirty-four-year-old waitress at Perkins, a casual dining chain that specialized in pancake breakfasts. The average-looking brunette gave details of a sexual relationship to the British tabloid *News of the World*. In an interview that surpassed the seediness of any previous allegations, Lawton claimed to have had sex with Tiger multiple times in 2006 and 2007, including one "frantic" tryst in a church parking lot. She alleged that Tiger would flirt with her when he brought his then-pregnant wife to the restaurant. "He was not one to express his feelings to me," she complained. "I was there for sex." Lawton's sister gave an explicit interview to the tabloid, claiming that the golfer had refused to wear a condom during the encounters. The allegations of unsafe sex sent reverberations throughout the media, as pundits accused Tiger of putting his wife's health at risk.

Cori Rist, a thirty-one-year-old divorced mother of a seven-year-old boy, soon came forward, claiming a physical relationship with Tiger that had lasted six months. "He was not happy at home with his wife," she told *The Today Show.* "He would stay there because she was pregnant and they were expecting their first child. Because of his reputation, he had to uphold that." Cori told the media that she had believed she was Tiger's only mistress, but soon she picked up signs he was cheating with others. She claimed to have caught him texting someone in the middle of the night and believed he was talking to another woman.

Jamie Jungers, a twenty-six-year-old model, upped the ante yet again, claiming to have had sex with Tiger on the night his father died. She said that Tiger had visited Earl Woods at a hospice just hours before he passed away. When Tiger returned home, he called Jungers and had her meet him at his home. She told tabloids that she was sitting next to him when he received the call that his beloved father had died. She claimed to have been beside him wearing nothing but a pair of panties. But there were some logistical problems to her story: Earl Woods had died in the morning, not at night, and he had died at home, not in a hospice. Still, her story spread throughout the media like wildfire, and pundits discussed the callousness of Tiger's proclivities.

The women continued to emerge: Playboy model Loredana Jolie said that Tiger had not limited his affairs to women; she claimed that he was bisexual. More women continued to come forward: porn stars Holly Sampson and Joslyn James, cocktail waitress Julie Postle, and Theresa Rogers, a fortysomething "cougar" who looked like an older version of Elin Nordegren. Four unidentified women were also rumored to have hired attorneys in anticipation of making public statements accusing the golfer of sexual relationships.

With the emergence of each additional woman, Elin grew angrier, confiding in friends that she wanted to make Tiger suffer for his indiscretions. It wasn't just the betrayal and the lies; now she was humiliated before the world. These women were going on television and sharing the most intimate details of their sex lives with her husband, yet no one seemed to care about her feelings. She called home to Sweden to draw on her family's comfort. Her mother, Barbro Holmberg, booked a flight to Florida and arrived on Monday afternoon, December 7. Tiger had left Orlando to stay with friends in the West Palm Beach area.

At 3:00 in the morning, less than twelve hours after Barbro had arrived, she collapsed in a downstairs bathroom. Panicked, Elin called 911.

Elin: Oh, my God. My mom just collapsed.

Operator: OK, calm down, OK, what is the address and is she breathing? They are coming.

Elin: (sobbing)

Operator: OK, calm down for a minute so that I can understand what's happening.

Elin: She collapsed in the bathroom. What do I do?

Operator: Is she breathing? Is she breathing?

Elin: Yeah, I just . . . just ran to the phone, hold on, hold on, hold on, hold on (children heard crying)

Elin: OK, she's fine.

Operator: Is she fine? It's OK, just calm down for me for a minute. OK, OK, and you said she collapsed?

Elin: Yeah.

Operator: OK. And how old is your mom?

Elin: Fifty . . . fifty-seven.

Operator: Fifty-seven? OK, you said she is breathing right?

Elin: Yeah.

Operator: Is she conscious?

Elin: Yes, she is.

Operator: OK, can you tell me what happened?

Elin: It's a hard line because I'm running back and forth from the phone.

Operator: OK, is there any way you can pick another phone and get as close to her as possible?

Elin: I'm gonna try, yeah, hold on. (Phone rings in distance.)

Elin: OK, she's fine.

Operator: You're saying she's fine?

Elin: Yes, she's talking to me.

Operator: Can she tell you what happened?

Elin: Yes, she said she collapsed and she fainted.

Operator: She fainted?

Elin: And she was down for a while. I heard her fall and then I ran in there and tried to get her up.

Operator: Is she injured from her fall?

Elin: I don't think so.

Operator: Is she bleeding from anywhere?

Elin: No.

Operator: OK. And has she not been feeling well or anything?

Elin: I don't know, I don't know.

Operator: And is her breathing completely normal?

Elin: Yeah.

Operator: Do you still want paramedics to come out?

Elin: No, I think we're fine, I'm sorry.

Operator: OK, can you tell me if she has any history of heart problems?

Elin: Hang on one second. . . . No.

Operator: I'm sorry?

Elin: No. I'm sorry. I got so scared.

Operator: That's OK, that's fine. We'd rather come check her and see, check her vitals and make sure that everything's OK.

Elin: OK. I think it's not urgent, though, now.

Operator: Is it OK if they come check her?

Elin: Yeah.

Operator: Just keep a close eye on her. Does she have a history of heart problems?

Elin: No.

Operator: Keep a close eye on her and if anything gets any worse call us right back OK?

Elin: I will. Thank you very much.

Operator: They'll be there in a few minutes.

Elin: It's a gated community.

Operator: OK, is there a code?

Elin: No, you can come right through.

For the second time in less than two weeks, an ambulance arrived on Deacon Circle in the early hours of the morning, its flashing lights piercing the darkness of the quiet community. Paramedics loaded Barbro onto a stretcher and started an IV. The ambulance made the familiar eight-mile trek to Health Central Hospital, admitting Barbro through the same doors that had opened for Tiger

44

just eleven days earlier. As she had done before, Elin followed after the ambulance in her own Escalade.

Composing herself, Elin parked her car and walked into the hospital lobby. "I'm looking for my mother," she calmly said to the worker at the information desk. "She was just brought in." When she was directed to the correct room, she managed a weak smile as she realized she'd be sitting in the same room where she had sat with her husband on the morning after Thanksgiving. Barbro was treated at the hospital and released the same afternoon; she would be fine.

On December 11, nearly two weeks after the accident, Tiger released another statement. It was the most candid he had been yet, explicitly admitting his infidelities for the first time.

I am deeply aware of the disappointment and hurt that my infidelity has caused to so many people, most of all my wife and children. I want to say again to everyone that I am profoundly sorry and that I ask forgiveness. It may not be possible to repair the damage I've done, but I want to do my best to try.

I would like to ask everyone, including my fans, the good people at my foundation, business partners, the PGA Tour, and my fellow competitors, for their understanding. What's most important now is that my family has the time, privacy, and safe haven we will need for personal healing.

After much soul searching, I have decided to take an indefinite break from professional golf. I need to focus my attention on being a better husband, father, and person.

Again, I ask for privacy for my family and I am especially grateful for all those who have offered compassion and concern during this difficult period.

Although the hiatus was expected, the announcement sent waves of shock and concern throughout the golf world. Tiger Woods had transformed the game by surpassing its barriers; he was its marquee star, the one who spiked ratings and turned the younger generation on to the game. His absence would be a blow to the sport. What would golf do without him?

Thanksgiving gave way to December, and the story of Tiger's infidelity continued to command the front page of daily newspapers as people read more about the icon whose image had shattered along with the windows of his Escalade.

Things got even worse for Tiger in mid-December when the Department of Children and Families confirmed that it had visited Tiger's house to check on the well-being of Tiger and Elin's children, Sam Alexis and Charlie Axel. DCF had received a tip on its tipline; by law, the department had to follow up. Two DCF officers, accompanied by a police escort, arrived at the house and spent nearly an hour questioning both Tiger and Elin. Although they found nothing amiss, the visit was humiliatingly splashed across newspaper headlines. There was just one curious detail: The foyer of the Woods home had suffered some unexplained damage; there were holes in the wall, and some of the artwork had clearly been removed.

On December 14, the *New York Times* reported on its Web site that Dr. Anthony Galea, a doctor who had treated Tiger at least four times with a blood-spinning technique after his knee surgery, was under suspicion of providing athletes with performance-enhancing drugs. The *Times* reported that Galea was being investigated by both the FBI and the Royal Canadian Mounted Police. Human growth hormone and Actovegin, a drug extracted from calf's blood, had reportedly been found in his medical bag at the U.S.-Canadian border in October. Because Actovegin is illegal in the United States, his assistant had been arrested and Galea was questioned. The *Times* reported that Tiger's agents at IMG, worried about his slow recovery, had referred him to Galea.

Galea quickly denied the claims. His attorney issued a statement on his behalf. "Dr. Galea was never engaged in any wrongdoing or any impropriety. We're confident that an investigation of

Dr. Galea will lead to his total vindication."

Mark Steinberg, who had previously been reticent about making public statements, quickly went on the offensive, widely issuing a statement to discredit the *Times* article. "The treatment Tiger received is a widely accepted therapy and to suggest some connection with illegality is recklessly irresponsible," Mark said. He continued, "The *New York Times* is flat wrong, no one at IMG has ever met or recommended Dr. Galea, nor were we worried about the progress of Tiger's recovery." The swiftness of Mark's response made one thing perfectly clear: Tiger Woods could survive a sex scandal, but he could not survive allegations of doping. His fans and sponsors would forgive him for cheating on his wife, but they would never forgive him for cheating on golf.

The last bomb to detonate under Tiger in December came the next day when his former high school girlfriend, Dina Gravell, told multiple media outlets that Tiger's father had been a cheater as well, carrying on numerous affairs while Tiger was still in high school. According to Dina, who had dated Tiger for three years, Tiger would call her in tears, devastated that Earl was betraying the family with his philandering.

It wasn't a surprising allegation, at least to certain members of the golfing community; writers had long whispered about Earl Woods's proclivities while on tour. But golf writers weren't paid to write about Earl's sex life; they were paid to cover the game. Whatever Earl had done throughout Tiger's career had been his own business as far as they were concerned, and the rumors of Earl's infidelity never reached a wide audience.

As Christmas 2009 approached, Tiger's image lay in ruins. Even Tiger's friends were left questioning themselves about the superstar they had known. How had this all happened to him? And, more importantly, did they really know Tiger Woods at all?

CHAPTER 2

EARL WOODS WAS A STORYTELLER always on the prowl for a new audience. It wasn't merely that he liked to hear himself talk; it was that he believed he had something to say—a lesson to teach the world—and the easiest way to get his point across was with a story. Before Tiger Woods became Tiger Woods, Earl's stories were often met with the polite smiles of an audience that was only half-listening. But once his son became an icon, the stories took on a certain gravitas, and Earl never again had trouble finding anyone to listen to him.

In reality, the forty-three years that Earl Woods lived before Tiger's birth were every bit as eventful as the thirty years that followed. Raising Tiger was Earl's second act, an illustrious ending to a life of achievement and adventure, racism and regrets. Earl didn't keep the first half of his life a secret—he was a man who profoundly believed in candidness—but he soon learned that the world was more interested in anecdotes about his life with his famous son. Everything that came before was unimportant, eclipsed by the legend of Tiger Woods, at least in the public consciousness.

The public ignorance of Earl's life didn't make it any less important to him—or to Tiger, who grew up hearing the stories and developed a comprehensive knowledge of the experiences that had shaped his father's life. When Tiger was very young, the stories could be a manipulative tool; he would ask his father for stories in the evening, knowing that the hour-long narrative could postpone bedtime. But as Tiger got older, he and Earl realized that these stories carried a profound significance to both of them. The stories bonded father and son together, helping Tiger to gain a deeper understanding of the man raising him and helping Earl to impart some wisdom to his son.

This is not to say that Earl was always accurate in his storytelling. Although he prided himself on his honesty, Earl was uninterested in the details, so his tales were often filled with contradictions and inconsistencies. The vagueness, especially Earl's inattention to dates and locations, infused an aura of mystery into the stories. Tiger accepted the inconsistencies easily, choosing to focus on the message and moral of the stories; these weren't tales where he asked a lot of questions. Other listeners weren't nearly as forgiving; it eventually became necessary for the media to fact-check Earl's stories with public records. He wasn't deliberately trying to mislead anyone; he simply didn't care about the minutiae.

ON MARCH 5, 1932, in the midst of the Great Depression's stranglehold on the American economy, Earl Woods was the youngest of six children born to a hardscrabble working-class family in Manhattan, Kansas. In addition to the era's considerable economic hardships, the southern plains were suffering from powerful storms that spewed black, blinding dust into the atmosphere, devastating farms and destroying livestock. The economic fallout rippled outward, swiftly and disproportionately affecting poor and minority families like the Woodses. The physical and figurative black cloud hovered over the family for years, resulting in chronic unemployment and poverty. Despite the external turmoil, the Woods family was close-knit, and Earl's arrival caused a mixture of delight and dismay. Although he was a healthy, happy baby, he was another mouth to feed, an additional responsibility for a family that had far more obligations than it had opportunities.

The tiny white clapboard house at 1015 Yuma Street was brand new when the Woods family bought it for $385 in 1921. Built in 1920, it had a full front porch and a good-sized front yard. Although the Woods family kept the home immaculate—fresh impatiens and marigolds surrounded the porch every spring—the house was still part of a poor, black neighborhood that was worlds removed from the affluent white suburbs just a few blocks away. Yuma Street was the type of road that few people ever escaped; they grew up there, lived their lives there, and died there.

Miles Woods had lived nearly sixty difficult years before his son Earl was born. In the early part of the twentieth century, he had eked out a modest living as a day laborer, a lumber delivery-man, and a trash hauler. As the Roaring Twenties gave way to the depressed thirties, Miles became a stonemason, a stable, yet grueling job with better hours and an $18 weekly salary. It was good money for the time, but still below the poverty line. Miles had been married before and had had five children with his first wife, and his parenting experience caused him to be rigid and unyielding. He was a strict father, one who demanded respect with his stern glances and sharp voice. His children simultaneously loved and feared him.

After the death of his first wife, Miles married Maude Carter in 1919. She was the daughter of a poor farmer from Leavenworth, Kansas. Twenty years younger than her husband, Maude was a striking biracial woman with light brown skin and soft features. She wore her graying hair in a tight bun, which gave her a look of competence and authority. Maude, who had been the first member of her family to attend college, was convinced that education and knowledge were the only way for her family to transcend its current situation. When Miles and Maude married, she made him promise that all of their children would be educated; it was a nonnegotiable condition of matrimony.

Earl's oldest brother, Miles Jr., was born in 1921, followed in short order by sisters Hastie Belle, Freda, Lillian, and Mabel. By the time Earl came along in 1932, the tiny house was bursting at the seams. There was no money to buy a bigger home —and nicer neighborhoods would not welcome a black family—but Miles was good at construction work; with the help of some relatives, he added a third bedroom to the small wood-frame home. The largest bedroom belonged to Miles and Maude. The girls shared the newest bedroom, while Earl bunked with his older brother. With eight people living in a 1,100-square-foot home, the family was close, both physically and emotionally. As with any family, there were squabbles over unimportant issues, but the Woods family was one cohesive unit; Maude and Miles saw to that.

The Woods household was a religious one; Miles was a staunch Baptist, and Maude was a Methodist. They lived a sedate, serious life of temperance and restraint—no alcohol, tobacco, or crude language was allowed within 1015 Yuma Street, and violations of the family strictures would result in severe spankings, usually at the hands of Maude, not Miles. She was the disciplinarian of the family, the one who was instrumental in teaching her children the difference between right and wrong. Even though Earl and his siblings didn't always do what was right, they credited Maude with teaching them manners, morals, and, most of all, obedience. Scripture memory was mandatory among all the children, but none of them knew as many Bible verses as Maude, who often quoted Proverbs 22:15:

"Foolishness is bound in the heart of a child, but the rod of correction shall drive it far from him."

Maude Carter Woods knew that her children were at a disadvantage, at least when it came to material possessions. They were poor and black, which automatically meant that they would have limited educational opportunities. Although she couldn't provide every material desire, she could instill a sense of pride and self-reliance in the Woods children. She would daily tell them that they were as good as anyone else, but that they would have to expend extra effort to prove their worth to small-minded people who judged them by their skin color. She had an aching desire to see them succeed, and Earl Woods, like his siblings, was expected to work hard, even when he was young. He had his schoolwork, of course, and his daily chores used up the rest of his time. To make ends meet, the family raised chickens in the backyard, and it was Earl's responsibility to feed them and clean their coops. He was also responsible for slaughtering them, a gory job that neither thrilled nor repulsed him. It was just what he had to do so that the family could eat.

There was little time for fun when Earl was young—life was too difficult to waste too many hours on recreational activities—but Earl eventually developed an obsession that would shape the rest of his early life. Miles Woods moonlighted as a scorekeeper for the baseball diamond near the family home, keeping stats for the white leagues that played on the field. Earl would hover outside the ballpark to catch the foul balls; with money so tight, it was the only way he could get baseballs to play with later.

On special occasions, the Negro League teams —including his father's favorite team, the Kansas City Monarchs—would come to town on one of their barnstorming tours. Miles pulled some strings and got Earl inside the ballpark, where he worked as a batboy. Earl was speechless as he met the players—although he would later spin elaborate tales of his interactions with baseball legends such as Satchel Paige, Bob Feller, and Roy Campanella in his repertoire of life stories. As he watched the games, Earl fell in love with the tangibles of the baseball diamond: the sight of the athletes, the cheers of the crowd, the feel of the fresh air.

Miles was a deliberate man, and his decisions were almost always intentional. He didn't merely want to expose Earl to baseball; he wanted to indoctrinate him into the sport. Miles knew that baseball could be a ticket out of Manhattan and into a fulfilling, relevant life, and he dreamed that his son would be able to use sports to overcome poverty.

"YOU NEED TO PLAY FOR THE MONARCHS when you grow up." It wasn't the beginning of a conversation; it was a sudden one-sentence decree that

Miles Woods announced to Earl at the dinner table.

"Okay, Dad," answered young Earl Woods, noticing his mother's arched eyebrow.

"After you finish school," Maude said firmly. "Remember, your education always comes first."

It was a lifelong disagreement between Miles and Maude Woods, a gentle tug-of-war over the children's futures. Whereas Miles wanted the boys to play baseball, Maude just wanted them to do their homework. She was fighting a losing battle.

Earl wasn't one to make a lot of concrete plans for his future; that was a skill he would develop later in life. As a child, he was an eternal dreamer, believing that things would always work out for him; he would somehow make something of himself. He didn't think of himself as being particularly optimistic; he just thought of himself as being ambitious. He would succeed, he'd tell himself, and nothing would stop him, no matter what the color of his skin.

Miles Woods knew that there were few career paths for blacks in that era, and he could see only one obstacle to Earl's future in baseball: the U.S. Army. Manhattan was the home of Fort Riley, a large U.S. Army installation that housed nearly 30,000 soldiers in the 1940s. Miles Woods would watch as the recruits cruised the downtown area, trying to hook up with pretty girls— including his daughters. He developed a distrust of soldiers; he knew what they were after, and he wanted no part of it for his family. He made Earl promise that he would never enlist; besides, Earl was going to play baseball for Miles's beloved Kansas City Monarchs.

Times weren't easy, and the Woodses faced a lot of challenges, but they were generally living happy, productive lives while Earl attended elementary school. Then, in 1943, when Earl was eleven, a tragedy struck that would forever change the family dynamic. For as long as Earl could remember, Miles had had health problems; he often had violent epileptic seizures that would cause him to injure himself as he thrashed on the floor. Miles's heart was failing, and years of hard work had worn out his back and shoulders. The unkind years piled up, and his body began to shut down as he aged. On one dreadful Saturday afternoon in August, Miles had a stroke and quickly died at home.

By this point, Earl's older brother was in the military—a decision that had caused a rift between the father and son—and Earl was the only male in the home. At the funeral, Maude Woods put her arm around Earl and drew her head close to his. "You're the man of the house now," she whispered. It was a statement that both excited and terrified Earl, who often cited that remark as the moment he grew up, shedding his boyish behavior and becoming a man.

Even when Miles was alive, there hadn't been much money in the Woods household. After his death, the money got even tighter. Earl continued to raise chickens as a supplemental way to feed the family, often selling extra fowl and eggs to neighbors and friends. Although Maude had a college degree, she was unable to find employment commensurate with her education. She finally took a job as a maid for a white family that wasn't as educated as she was. It destroyed her spirit, Earl believed, but he noted that she never once complained, at least not to him.

Earl instinctively knew that things couldn't keep going this way forever; the family that had previously been happy and poor was now simply poor. Days would go by without Maude smiling; she was inconsolable, not only about Miles's death, but also about the changes in her life. Two years later, when Earl was a thirteen-year-old eighth grader, his mother died suddenly of a stroke at age fifty-four. Earl would later say that she died of a broken heart; she simply didn't want to live without Miles. Earl would also say that he wasn't surprised about Maude's death—he had been watching her waste away for nearly two years.

Losing parents alters a person in a way that those with living parents can't comprehend, and the transformation becomes more acute the younger the person is when orphaned. Earl responded to his personal tragedies by becoming self-sufficient, a boy who could take on the responsibilities of a man. If he had been living in different circumstances, he might have run wild, but there were few opportunities for him to act out in Manhattan, Kansas. Besides, he hadn't been raised that way.

Although there was initially some discussion about what should happen to Earl and his siblings, the family soon figured out the most logical solution. His oldest sister, Hastie ("Hattie") Belle, was a schoolteacher in her twenties. She, with her husband, Jesse, would move into the small clapboard home on Yuma Street, becoming a surrogate parent to her own siblings. Although Hattie was a loving disciplinarian, she couldn't take the place of their mother in Earl's heart, and he continued to grieve for his lost parents for the rest of high school.

THERE WASN'T MUCH MONEY FOR COLLEGE, at least not in the traditional way. Earl wanted to continue his education, but he was realistic about his opportunities: He wasn't going to find a job that paid enough for him to attend classes, and getting an academic scholarship was out of the question. The only thing that Earl had going for him was his baseball ability.

Somehow, Earl was accepted at Kansas State University; he would forever maintain that he received a baseball scholarship, even though the facts didn't support the claim and the school had no record of offering him any assistance. The campus was just five minutes from his house; he could ride his bicycle to classes.

Earl somehow managed to find the money he

needed to attend school; he chose sociology as a major and psychology as a minor. He wasn't a great student, but he fulfilled the requirements to pass all his classes. He was more interested in baseball than in academics, and he saw his future on the diamond.

As the team's catcher, Earl was the only black player on the team, as well as the first black baseball player in the (then) Big Seven conference. It was a visible position on a prominent team, but Earl didn't find the attention to be anything new. His high school had been predominantly white, so he was used to standing out. What he wasn't prepared for was the verbal abuse he would receive as the player closest to the crowd. During every game, he was subjected to a steady stream of racial slurs and harassment from the crowd, and he noticed something surprising: It wasn't just the opposing team's fans who would toss out epithets; even the home crowd would call him a "nigger" if he made a bad play. He determined to intently focus through the experience, tuning out the taunts as he concentrated on the game. More importantly, Earl realized that he had to succeed; failure would always result in people, even those who considered themselves his friends, turning their backs on him. The taunting would become another learning experience in a youth full of harsh life lessons.

Earl Woods finished his freshman year with a grade point average of 2.1, his report card littered with Cs and Ds. He knew that his grades weren't great; he skipped classes and spent all his free time on the baseball field. As the spring semester drew to a close, his grades sank even further, and he found himself on academic probation. During the summer break, Earl was given an agonizing choice: The Kansas City Monarchs offered him a chance to turn pro, a big break for the nineteen-year-old. His salary would be $120 a month, more than his father had ever made. It would be his father's dream, and the idea of posthumously honoring his father appealed to Earl. As he mulled over the offer, he remembered his mother's admonition: to stay in school, no matter what the cost. Going pro would be the end of Earl's education, and despite his thin promises to himself to return to college after he was done playing major league baseball, he knew he would never finish his degree.

"That was a difficult decision for me," Earl would say later. "It was probably the hardest thing I had ever had to do up to that point. I was giving up my dream for the dream of my mother's. She wanted me to go to college, and I did. It might have cost me, but it was worth it.

"When you're young, there's always a feeling like it's now or never," he continued. "I felt like if I didn't go to college then, I'd never go to college. Now I wonder if I could have done both. But it all worked out. Things happen for a reason."

Earl spent several excruciating days weighing

his options. Was he cut out for college? After all, he wasn't anywhere close to graduating with honors. It would certainly be fun to play baseball, but what would he do after his athletic career was done? Would he have fewer opportunities if he dropped out of college?

With his mother's voice in the back of his head, Earl reluctantly passed on the opportunity, effectively turning his back on any chance to play professional baseball. For days, he thought of little else but his decision, wondering whether he had made the right choice or whether he had thrown away his only chance of success. As he was returning to Kansas State University the following September, he had an epiphany: If he sacrificed his dream of professional baseball for his education, then he would need to do better in his academic work. He started studying more, attending classes, and completing his homework. His grades started to improve.

Despite his extra effort in the classroom, Earl refused to forsake the sport he loved so much. He returned to the baseball diamond during his second year with a renewed ambition to be the best catcher that Kansas State had ever seen. His sophomore year would be his best year, both academically and competitively, as Earl determined to prove to himself that he hadn't made a mistake. The Kansas State team traveled across the Midwest for their away games, with Earl often driving some of his teammates around in his black Ford.

. . .

"IS HE WITH YOU?" The motel manager had lowered his voice to a near whisper. The Kansas State University team wanted to check into a nondescript roadside motel near Oklahoma City, and the manager had just noticed Earl in the parking lot.

The baseball coach, standing in front of the check-in window, immediately knew what the issue was but decided that playing dumb might be the best plan. "I'm Ray Wauthier," he said, speaking through the circular cutout in the office window. "What seems to be the problem?"

"Well, um, we have a rule here," the manager told Coach Wauthier. "We just don't allow coloreds to stay here." He was clearly embarrassed to be saying this; even when exclusion is the norm, it is often difficult to verbalize. Some of Earl's teammates were in earshot of the uncomfortable conversation, and they looked at the ground in embarrassment. Earl continued to stand by his car, no doubt aware of the drama unfolding a few yards away.

"I see," Coach Wauthier replied. "So are you willing to lose all of our business by not letting one of my players stay here?"

"Yes, sir, I am," the motel manager said. "Those are the rules. But there's a motel for coloreds about three miles from here. He can stay there while you stay here."

Coach Wauthier thought for a minute. "I think we'll try our luck somewhere else," he said, calling the manager's bluff. "If the whole team can't stay here, then none of us will stay here."

"Well," said the manager, slowly, "I guess I can check in everyone else. We don't have any rules against our guests having visitors. Maybe he's just a visitor, and maybe I don't see him. What I don't know won't hurt me, right?"

"No, I think we'll go somewhere else," Coach Wauthier said as team members got back into their cars and drove off.

Nowhere was Earl's race more apparent than when he traveled with his baseball team for away games. Many restaurants refused to serve him, and the ones that did often relegated him to the kitchen while his teammates ate in the dining room. When the team would take a bus to away games, Earl had to sit in back. The bigotry was frustrating and demoralizing to Earl, who found it difficult to bond with his teammates in these situations. The racism stuck with Earl, and he would later tell these stories when Tiger encountered racism on the PGA Tour. The stories of his baseball career would become an integral part of Earl's life narrative, and they became especially interesting to Tiger.

"I would tell Tiger a lot of stories about the racism I had to deal with," Earl would later say. "I think it's important for him to know that things haven't always been like they are now. There were a lot of troubles that we all had to deal with, stuff that he wouldn't understand unless I told him. It was very important to me that he knew the struggles that I went through."

Black college graduates in the early 1950s had two career paths after finishing college. They could work for the post office, alongside whites with high school degrees, or they could go into the military. Earl didn't want to enlist; he remembered his father's distaste for the military and didn't want to go against his father's wishes again. He was still haunted by his decision to let a baseball career pass him by; he couldn't bear to think of what his father would have said to his military career.

But Earl had more to worry about than Miles's wishes. He was in love with Barbara Hart, a pretty young woman with a quick wit and infectious smile. Earl had marriage on his mind, but he was concerned about providing for her; his father had taught him the importance of working hard to support a family, and Earl wouldn't consider marriage until he was financially ready.

ONCE EARL WAS DONE WITH COLLEGE, he felt it was time to walk down the aisle. In May 1954, just months after receiving his Bachelor of Science in Sociology, Earl and Barbara married in a very simple ceremony. A month after the wedding, Earl, then twenty-two, enlisted in the U.S. Army. Although he wasn't used to being told what to do, he eventually adapted to the structure and discipline of the military. He didn't like the rigidity, but he enjoyed the interaction with the other soldiers. Just days after enlisting, he felt an overwhelming peace in his new surroundings, as if he had finally discovered his destiny. "I knew it was for me," he would later say. "I was part of something great."

EVERYONE WAS STARING. It was hard for Earl not to notice the people gawking at him and his pretty young wife. At first, he thought they were staring at him because they thought he was handsome, but there was something in the way the people looked at him that made him realize that something strange was going on.

It was 1955, and Earl was stationed in Germany. Barbara had come with him, and the young couple started looking for a place to live. They met with a landlord in downtown Bern to show them apartments.

The crowd formed suddenly, before Earl even knew what was happening. He turned to the landlord. "They're staring at us like we're exhibits at the zoo," he said. "Why are they doing that?"

The landlord looked down at his feet; he didn't want to address the question, and he struggled for a moment before coming up with an answer. "They're looking for your tails," he whispered.

Earl stared at him in amazement. "Our tails?"

"When the white soldiers came here for World

War II," the landlord replied, "they told everyone that black people had tails."

The conversation bothered Earl, and the
memory of this disconcerting incident stayed with
him for the rest of his life. It didn't especially
trouble him that the Germans would believe that
blacks had tails, but it baffled him that white
American soldiers, who had served alongside
black soldiers in the trenches of war, would tell
such racist lies.

EARL WOODS HAD NEVER BEEN a perfect father,
and he was always the first one to acknowledge
his many shortcomings. Barbara soon got pregnant and delivered a baby boy in 1955. They
named him Earl "Denny" Woods Jr. Denny was a
strong, healthy boy, and Earl was overwhelmed
with fatherly pride, but his military service kept
him away from home, and he missed many of
Denny's milestones. The first tooth, the first word,
the first step: These were events that Denny celebrated with his mother alone. Two years later,
Barbara gave birth to another boy; they named
him Kevin Dale Woods. A daughter, Royce
Renay, was born in 1958.

To all outward appearances, Earl seemed to be
living the best dream that a black man could hope
for before the Civil Rights Act was adopted in
1964. He was on the upward track in the military,
with a beautiful wife and three healthy children.

But Earl was living a life of inner regret; his marriage was anything but happy. He and Barbara argued frequently: He thought she was too demanding; she thought he was cruel and pompous. The requirements of military life kept him far away from home; his children didn't know him and seldom got to spend time with him. It bothered Earl that he could succeed in his career, yet lose the people who should matter most to him.

After a yearlong tour of Vietnam, Earl returned to the States in February 1963 to see his family. He arrived home and tried to hug Royce, only to have the little girl pull back from him. "I remember coming back from one tour of Vietnam, and my daughter answered the door and wondered who I was," said Earl regretfully. "Because of my military responsibilities, I just wasn't there for my first family. We were strangers."

His failure as a father to his first children always stung, a reminder that he was an imperfect man. If he had to do it again, he thought, he'd be an attentive, hands-on father who spent time with his children, teaching them skills and sports while instilling life lessons. He wanted another chance.

But it was too late to reclaim the lost years with his family, and besides, Earl's relationship with Barbara was rapidly deteriorating. Arguments pushed them further apart, and as they drifted away from each other, they stopped feeling like a married couple. Barbara was responsible for the children's daily needs, and she became the only parent the three really knew.

By the late 1960s, Earl's relationship with Barbara was over; they were living independent lives: she with the children and he with the military. When Earl and Barbara sat down in late 1967 to discuss their futures, there was no anger or yelling. There was simply the sober countenance of two people heavy with their own history and, once again, with issues to discuss: his absenteeism, her resentment. As they sat in the living room of their home, they both acknowledged that there was only one conclusion that would make sense, that would give them any sense of normalcy: It was time to separate.

Although the separation might have been traumatic for many children, the three Woods children took the development with the flexibility and stoicism that often accompany the children of parents who decide too late that they can no longer live together. After all, all three children were already living apart from their father; they would notice no real difference. They saw him infrequently, and each time they spoke with him, Earl felt that he had to reacquaint himself with his own children. This was a separation, not a divorce, although both Earl and Barbara acknowledged the direction in which their relationship was ultimately headed. But for now, they would just spend some time apart.

Years later, Earl would draw Barbara's ire when he characterized his marriage to her as a mulligan, a tragic mistake that he regretted—as if he had received no benefit from the union. The media would notice that he called his first three children a trial run for his true destiny, which was being Tiger's father. The denigration of the marriage stung Barbara, and she later wrote a tell-all book that accused Earl of being cruel and distant. The resentment would linger for a lifetime, and even decades later Barbara would claim that Earl had betrayed her.

The media weren't covering the Woods family in the 1960s, so the pain of the splintering marriage was kept between Earl, Barbara, and the three children. The family would never be a cohesive unit again, if it had ever been one in the first place. Barbara remained in the family house and took care of the children while Earl went off to search for his next adventure.

In 1968, Earl headed to Fort Bragg, North Carolina. Now thirty-five, he was approaching midlife with the concerns of a man who was noticing his body just beginning to slow down. For years, Earl had wanted to become a Green Beret; the discipline and physical prowess of the Green Berets impressed and intrigued him, and he wanted to prove to himself that he had what it took to become one. Believing that the Green Berets were a bastion of equality, where each man would be judged on merit rather than on skin color, Earl attended the grueling boot camp with men who were more than a decade younger than he was. Refusing to be intimidated by his age, Earl determined to pace himself with the younger soldiers: stride for stride, pushup for pushup. Mentally steeling himself, Earl determined that the physical challenges were all in his head; if he could just concentrate and focus, he could do anything that the other men could do. He actually enjoyed the demanding physical training, plane jumping, and cross-country hikes, despite the toll they took on his body. Determined to succeed, Earl managed to keep up with the rest of the men; although he was constantly in pain, he was pushing himself further than he had ever thought possible . . . and he was succeeding. It was an all-encompassing undertaking, distracting Earl from the pain and guilt of his separation from Barbara; it was precisely what he needed. Six months later, he was qualified as a Green Beret commander in a ceremony he would later call one of the proudest of his life.

There was no overwhelming need for Earl to get married again, at least not in his mind. He was still young and handsome, with a natural charisma that attracted women; he had no shortage of female companionship. His military career was going well; he was enjoying promotions and pay increases, maybe not at the rate of his white colleagues, but he still felt that he was doing well. Earl had been tied down before; he knew the regret that came with a military relationship. Why would he do that to a woman—and, more importantly, to himself—unless it was absolutely necessary?

Later in 1968, Earl received his newest orders: He would be stationed in Bangkok, Thailand, nearly 8,000 miles away from his wife and children's home in California. It was a big step up: He would be a special services officer, responsible for coordinating the leisure activities of all the soldiers on the base. It was during his year in Bangkok that he would meet Kultida, a pretty young Thai woman who would change his life forever.

CHAPTER 3

SHE WAS BEAUTIFUL, Earl thought. Not a lot of makeup, no fancy clothes. She was simple, yet breathtakingly beautiful. With her waist-length jet-black hair, flawless skin, and perfect teeth, the diminutive Thai woman was among the most stunning women Earl Woods had ever seen. He had never believed in love at first sight—he wasn't sure if he believed in it now—but he couldn't deny how attracted he was to her. She looked him in the eye—something that was shockingly rare for Earl in 1968—and her eyes twinkled as she spoke to him. He extended his hand, and she shook it gently, yet purposefully, which Earl thought conveyed a certain self-confidence he didn't often see among the women in Bangkok. Many women would look down when they talked to Earl, as if they were ashamed of him—or themselves for talking to him. But if this woman was self-conscious, she certainly didn't show it, and her self-assurance was appealing to Earl.

If she had never met Earl Woods, Kultida Punsawad probably would have married very well in Thailand. She came from a highly regarded family. Her father, Vit Punsawad, was an architect who also owned a tin mine that employed dozens of miners; her mother was a teacher. Her extended family owned several businesses, including a fleet of buses in Bangkok. Everyone in the family was educated; everyone was ambitious. It was a family without black sheep, at least none that anyone knew about. Kultida was part of this marrying stock: educated, intelligent, and, most importantly, respectable.

The importance of coming from a reputable family cannot be overstated, especially in the rigid social strata of 1960s Thailand. Kultida—or "Tida," as most of her friends called her—was the marrying kind, a woman that any Thai man would have been proud to take home to mother. She probably would have married a successful businessman or even a government minister, and her husband would have been congratulated on finding such a gracious and dignified wife. She could help cement her family's social status if she married the right man and could destroy it if she married the wrong one.

Kultida was born in 1944 in the province of Kanchanaburi, about seventy-five miles northwest of Bangkok. Growing up in the shadow of the newly built and yet to be immortalized bridge on the River Kwai, she was an independent spirit who said what she thought and didn't back down from a fight. She had always been small for her age—shorter than the other girls—and she topped out at five feet tall. What Kultida lacked in stature, she compensated for by being aggressive, opinionated, and surprisingly self-assured. She was the type who would say what was on her mind, no matter the consequences. There were no apologies later, because her words were a reflection of how she was feeling at the time. What she lacked in tact, she made up for in loyalty and protectiveness, making her a trusted confidante for girls her age.

Kultida's parents divorced when she was five (she was the youngest of four children), and she was sent off to boarding school while her parents figured things out. For the next five years, she saw the family only on holidays and during vacations while getting a superior education that was out of reach for many Thai girls. The education was no consolation for her separation from her family, and Kultida was often miserable so far from home.

Boarding school is an isolating place, and Kultida often fought overwhelming feelings of abandonment. Each weekend, she'd hold out hope that her family would visit, to tell her that she was loved and needed. Each weekend, no one would come, and Kultida would spend the long days wondering why her parents had deserted her.

At age ten, she left boarding school and was shuttled between her father's and her mother's homes. By then, both parents had remarried. There were new children in their lives, children who lived with them, and Kultida wondered why she had been replaced. Her stepparents compounded her isolation, speaking to her infrequently and superficially. It was a lonely childhood in which

Kultida had to learn to fend for herself; she became her own source of strength. Her faith in Buddhism gave her an inner peace that carried her.

There were many drawbacks to Kultida's time at boarding school, but she also gained a valuable skill that would shape the rest of her life. In addition to learning the basics (math, reading, and science), Kultida learned to speak English, an ability that would ensure her gainful employment as an adult and help guide her destiny.

In the late 1960s, Kultida was suffering from her own form of discrimination. Jobs were difficult for women to find; despite her education and intelligence, Kultida was relegated to support positions and menial jobs. In 1966, she found a job as a civilian secretary at the joint U.S.-Thai command in Bangkok, a job that she soon grew to love.

One of her family's biggest worries was that Kultida liked to fraternize with American soldiers. By today's standards, her behavior would have been considered fairly innocent—just a conversation here and there—but her parents would continually worry about her increasing contact with Americans. Women of her social class were encouraged to stay among themselves, not hang out with American soldiers, and certainly not with black ones.

Although the story of Earl and Kultida conjures up a scene from a romantic comedy, Earl always insisted that his account of meeting Kultida was completely true, even if the details may have gotten fuzzy over time. As a special services officer, Earl coordinated leisure activities for more than 100,000 soldiers. It was a position of great importance and visibility, and Earl reveled in the responsibility. He was in charge of sizable infrastructure needs, including the building and staffing of bowling alleys, baseball diamonds, and movie theaters. He hired civilian workers—between 500 and 4,000 of them, depending on when he was telling the story—and worked closely with local employers to find the right personnel.

In the late 1960s, it was unusual for a black man to have such immense responsibility in the military, and Earl developed a swagger that made the women notice him. He had something to prove, and he instinctively knew that he had to project an aura of confidence.

As rare as it was for a black military man to have such a responsibility, it was even less common for him to have a white assistant. In that era, blacks with administrative responsibility were usually given black assistants. Some white soldiers were reluctant to report to a black man, so the army minimized any possible controversies. But Earl's assistant was a blue-eyed, white soldier from the Midwest, which confused people who saw them together.

Earl and his assistant were looking for laborers in 1968 when they walked into the office where

Kultida was working. They needed to speak to her boss, and they arrived unannounced. As they walked into the office, Kultida stood up and approached the two men. Looking at the assistant, and ignoring Earl, she politely asked, "Can I help you, sir?" The assistant looked uncomfortably at Earl and then back at Kultida. "We're here to see the personnel officer," he replied uncertainly.

"Go right in," replied Kultida, still not looking at Earl.

More bemused than offended, Earl boldly strode into the personnel officer's office, followed by his assistant and Kultida. As they sat down, Earl grandiosely and brazenly propped his feet up on a coffee table, sending a message to Kultida that he, not his assistant, was in charge.

Mortified, Kultida instantly realized her mistake and tried to explain herself. "Oh, I'm so sorry," she stammered. "I didn't know you were in charge. I didn't mean anything by it."

"That's fine," Earl replied with a sly smile. "It's understandable. You've seen a lot of American movies." Earl masked his flirting as absolution; he wasn't offended, but he could score a few points by pretending to be forgiving.

After the meeting with the personnel officer was over, Earl and Kultida stood outside the office and chatted for a few minutes. Earl, who would later say that sparks flew between the two, asked her for a date. Despite the cultural expectations imposed on both of them, Kultida, surprisingly, agreed to meet him. They would meet at a restaurant; it would be improper for any man to meet her at her home. They settled on a time: 9:00.

With the excitement of a first date looming, Earl headed back to the barracks, stopping only to brag to some of his friends that he had gotten a date with a pretty girl. He showered, shaved, and changed into dress clothes and got to the restaurant at 9:00 that night, convinced that it would be a good night with a pretty lady.

But the night ended in disaster. First 9:00 came. Then 9:30. Then 10:00. Kultida didn't arrive, and she didn't call the restaurant to cancel the date. At 10:30, an annoyed and embarrassed Earl left the restaurant, having never been stood up before. He returned to his barracks and went to bed.

The next morning, Earl reported to work, still stinging from the previous night's rejection. Around 10:00 a.m., a secretary walked into his office. "The restaurant called and said that two young ladies are waiting for you," she said. "They're angry because you're late."

Earl hurried to the restaurant and found Kultida and a chaperone impatiently waiting. Kultida looked annoyed.

"Where in the hell were you last night?" Earl demanded.

Kultida looked at him quizzically. "What do you mean, 'last night'?"

"I said nine," huffed Earl.

"I was here at nine," Kultida shot back. "Where were you?"

Earl and Kultida stared at each other for a few seconds, each trying to figure out where their communications had broken down. Slowly, it dawned on them both that their cultural differences had led to diverging expectations. He had planned on a dinner date; she thought they were meeting for breakfast. After all, it would be improper for a Thai girl to meet a man at night. Nighttime dates were for prostitutes, not for a respectable girl like her. Dates should occur in the daylight hours, and a chaperone should accompany the couple; this was only proper.

Although the first date hadn't materialized, at least not in the way Earl had hoped, the attraction grew between Earl and Kultida. She liked his confidence, and how self-assured he was to ask her out on a date. He found her virtue appealing; she was a woman with a good head on her shoulders. That weekend, they went on their first real date—to a Thai church. Of course, a chaperone accompanied them; otherwise the date wouldn't have been proper.

Typically, when American soldiers are stationed overseas, relationships with foreigners can blossom quickly and move along swiftly. A sense of urgency spurs on these relationships, and taking it slow is simply not an option. Such romances can lead to one of two outcomes: Either the couple marries and the woman leaves her homeland, or the relationship is short-lived and the two go their separate ways. Within weeks of their first date, Earl and Kultida started dating frequently, always during the day, and their relationship soon grew from infatuation to devotion. Earl asked Kultida to marry him; she readily accepted.

Kultida returned to the States with Earl, and the couple married in Brooklyn in 1969. Technically, however, Earl was still married to Barbara, at least as far as U.S. law was concerned. Earl and Barbara had gotten a divorce in Mexico the year before, but they didn't divorce in the United States until 1972, when Barbara filed papers in Orange County, California. Earl felt that his marriage to Barbara had ended with their separation several years earlier; he saw no conflict in marrying Kultida. Despite the questionable dates, Earl and Kultida were registered as being legally married in the state of New York; their marriage license was filed with Kings County without any holdup. In later life, Earl would be deliberately fuzzy about the wedding dates in an attempt to confuse any nosy reporters about the status of his marriage.

PREDICTABLY, KULTIDA'S FAMILY was not pleased with her marriage, and Earl became a popular topic of derisive conversation among her extended family. Marrying a foreigner was shameful enough, but Earl wasn't just any foreigner; he was a black man. Some members of Kultida's family turned their backs on her, convinced that she had dishonored her family. But Kultida was in love, and she decided she didn't care what her family thought; Earl was her husband, and she would live her life with him.

But Earl and Kultida got an unexpected vote of confidence after they returned to the States. Vit Punsawad, Kultida's father, sent her a letter. He wasn't satisfied with the way his son, Kultida's brother, was raising his own son. Vit asked his daughter if she and Earl would take the grandson and raise him properly to be a man. The boy lived with Earl and Kultida for three years, eventually returning to Thailand more mature and mannerly. It was a watershed event in the relationship between Kultida and her family; family members now approved of Earl—maybe not as they would have accepted a respectable Thai man, but their reluctant acceptance was good enough for Kultida.

EARL HAD NEVER BEEN EXPOSED to Buddhism; there were no Buddhists in Manhattan, Kansas, or at least none that he had known of. His upbringing had been decidedly and devoutly Christian. He wasn't going to convert to Buddhism; it just wasn't for him. But he quickly learned to respect the positive aspects of the religion. Many American soldiers of the era would force their new brides to convert to Christianity, believing it would be easier to raise children in one religion. Earl respected Buddhism enough to allow Kultida to remain Buddhist; besides, he knew that it was impossible to convince her to do anything she didn't want to do. She didn't need his permission to remain Buddhist; she would keep her religion whether he liked it or not.

Earl and Kultida returned to America and began the nomadic life of an army officer's family. By 1972, they had moved to downtown Brooklyn, and Earl was stationed at Fort Hamilton, where he worked as a public relations officer. It was here that he learned vital lessons in dealing with the press. Answer only the question asked, offering no additional information needlessly. Manage the media meticulously, ensuring that every word is carefully planned. Recognize that reporters are not friends; they are looking for information that a respondent might not be willing to share. During the next year, Earl enjoyed playing crafty games of cat and mouse with local newspaper reporters; it became a sport to him, and it helped him sharpen his media skills. They would come in handy later.

In 1974, after Earl had spent twenty years in the army, he knew it was time to retire. He had served two tours in Vietnam and had been stationed on three continents. Now forty, he was ready to enter civilian life with Kultida. He would retire as a lieutenant colonel, receiving a good pension. The couple moved to California to be closer to Earl's children, buying a modest three-bedroom, two-bathroom home in Cypress.

THE ROCK SAILED through the kitchen window, startling Earl and Kultida as pieces of glass clattered to the floor. They had been in the all-white neighborhood in Cypress for just a few days; she already knew their arrival was not viewed positively among the neighbors, that someone didn't like them. She had noticed the dislike in the faces of the people on the street. She and Earl weren't white. They were different. And they weren't welcome.

But the rock incident shook her; it troubled her that people were so unhappy, so hateful, that they would resort to vandalizing the house of someone who had never done anything to them. Earl got the window fixed right away, but the memory remained with Kultida. She would have to teach her children the importance of accepting everyone, no matter the color of a person's skin.

"It bothered me that we were in the 1970s and I had to deal with this crap," Earl said in 2004, his eyes flashing with annoyance and anger. "We were supposed to be beyond that; America was supposed to become color blind, but it didn't happen. It was a lesson to my wife that it happened; she thought everything was fine here in America. It was a wake-up call."

The rock incident aside, Earl and Kultida settled into Cypress nicely. Earl took a job as a contract administrator and materials manager at McDonnell Douglas, then a major aerospace manufacturer and defense contractor. Their house was always full of people. One by one, each of Earl's kids with Barbara came to stay with him around their eighteenth birthday; they spent time getting to know their father, and the emotional distance between them shrank. Earl welcomed his children into the home, excited to have a second chance at connecting with them; it was a way to erase some of the regret.

The Woodses settled down as a family. But being a stepmother wasn't enough for Kultida; she was nearing thirty, and she longed for a child of her own. Under Thai customs, her marriage to Earl would never be truly consummated until they had a child; she tried to persuade Earl that they should have a baby.

Earl wasn't convinced, at least not immediately. He had his three children already, and he hadn't been there for them. He was forty-three years old now; did he really want to go through the midnight feedings and diaper phase? He thought about it, and he just wasn't sure that he wanted to become a new father again in his early forties. But he loved Kultida—more, he would later say, than he had ever loved his first wife—and he wanted to make her happy. He agreed to try for a baby.

By the spring of 1975, Kultida was pregnant. She was ecstatic; Earl, however, was ambivalent but generally pleased, and he grew more excited as the year wore on. As they bought baby supplies—a crib, a playpen, tiny clothes—Earl made a decision that this child would be his chance to right the wrongs he had made with his first three children. He would spend time with this child, perhaps find a hobby they could do together. Earl would not be an absentee father, not this time. He was sure of that.

Halloween passed, then Thanksgiving and Christmas, and the pregnancy went according to plan. Kultida dreamed up names for the baby. If the baby was a boy, she would call him Eldrick, a name she had invented. The first letter was an E, for Earl. The last letter was a K, for Kultida. The middle name would be a traditional Thai name, Tont.

She went into labor during the night and was rushed to the hospital. On the evening of December 30, 1975, Eldrick Tont Woods was born.

Shortly after young Eldrick Woods made his entrance into the world, a doctor came into the hospital room where Kultida lay, bearing some devastating news. Something was wrong, he said. The baby was fine, but Kultida was facing some reproductive issues; she would not be able to have more children. This would be the lone chance for Earl and Kultida to raise a boy into a man. They would have to do it right the first time.

CHAPTER 4

HE WAS BORN TO A FATHER WHO would describe him as the Chosen One, a boy who would grow into a man with the power to affect nations. His mother would call him the Universal Child, blessed with the ability to hold the races together. But on the evening of December 30, 1975, Eldrick Tont Woods was just another newborn baby in Cypress, California.

Earl had not been present for the delivery of his three older children with Barbara Woods; there had always been somewhere to go and something to do. He regretted being an absentee father, a man who had always put his own career and desires ahead of his responsibilities to his first family. Sure, he had supported his wife and children materially, ensuring that there was always a roof over their heads and food on the table, but even he would admit that he hadn't been there for them, not physically or emotionally.

But this baby was different, at least to Earl, and he did all the requisite fatherly duties: coaching Kultida in prenatal Lamaze classes, driving her to the hospital, and, most importantly, being present in the delivery room. Way before Eldrick was born, Earl felt an overwhelming sense of responsibility to him.

Earl couldn't really explain what made him so

devoted to this baby; if he understood his reasons, he was unwilling or unable to articulate them. He was now forty-three, with enough of his life behind him to understand the importance of being an attentive father. Earl liked to say that he sensed that something would be different about this child, that he would eventually become one of the greatest men to walk the earth. Perhaps that was the reason for Earl's attentiveness, or perhaps he had simply gained the maturity that comes with getting older.

Earl Woods was not an emotional man, and his stoicism accompanied him into the delivery room. He watched the events unfold with a clinical eye, fascinated at the process but feeling little emotion. He would later attribute his detached observations to his military training, which he believed gave him the ability to focus on the mechanics of an event, divorcing it from any emotion and sentiment.

Earl's emotional reaction to the birth was delayed, and the next day he was overwhelmed by the realization that he had been profoundly moved while watching the birth. Holding his day-old son in his arms, he choked back tears as he fulfilled a promise he had made to himself years earlier. Eldrick would be nicknamed after Colonel Vuong Dang "Tiger" Phong, a South Vietnamese officer whom Earl had befriended during the war. Eldrick would have big shoes to fill; to hear Earl tell it, Tiger Phong was an exemplary man who had saved Earl's life in combat multiple times. From this moment forward, Eldrick would be known as Tiger Woods.

The stories of Tiger's childhood would become the stuff of legend, every move documented by a proud father who believed that God had entrusted him with this baby for a higher purpose. More than a father, Earl was a trustee for this boy, a caretaker charged with raising him into an exceptional man. Each decision had to be inspired, had to reflect a commitment to be a good steward of what the Almighty had given Earl and Kultida.

Everyone has different parenting styles and expectations, especially when parents come from different cultures, as Earl and Kultida did. Shortly after Tiger's birth, they sat down at their kitchen table and discussed their philosophy of parenting. Earl wanted to be Tiger's best friend, sharing time and memories together. Kultida took a more utilitarian approach. She wanted to raise an educated, smart boy who was polite and ambitious. It was a long discussion, but Earl and Kultida Woods quickly realized they were on the same page: They would give everything they had to Tiger, sacrificing their own needs and desires for him. Tiger would be their top priority; he would always come first. On a practical level, Earl and Kultida decided that they would not hire babysitters. Parenting was a twenty-four-hour a day job. They agreed that one of them would always be responsible for watching Tiger. There was no way that they were going to leave the raising of this child to strangers. It wouldn't be easy, they realized, but this was a boy who was bound for greatness. They had a responsibility to nurture and train him. They would not let him down.

Earl had started playing golf when he left the army, and to hear him tell it, he had become quite good at the game. He couldn't play at all the courses in Southern California; many of them were reserved for white golfers. But he managed to pick up the sport quickly, and he developed a very strong swing. His long game was very good, but he would always admit that his putting needed a lot of work.

Summer 1976 was an unusually rainy summer in Cypress. El Niño was parked over the Pacific Ocean, resulting in soggy, waterlogged weeks when the sun would rarely make an appearance over Southern California. Earl wanted to play golf as he missed being on the fairways. Besides, Tiger was going stir-crazy inside the house; the nine-month-old wanted to be outside.

It would eventually become the bedrock of the Tiger Woods legend, a story that would be passed down so often that the details would change as the story evolved. Earl cleared out a part of the cluttered garage to create a makeshift putting range so that he could practice his swing. Placing Tiger in his white high chair, Earl would chip balls into a cup while his son watched, his eyes wide with fascination. There was something about the golf swing that fascinated Tiger. He didn't just watch it; he studied it, analyzing the way Earl moved.

After several days of being watched by Tiger, an amused Earl gave Tiger a child-sized golf club. As Tiger gripped the club, Earl watched in amazement as Tiger swung it perfectly, precisely mimicking his father's movements. With the exuberance of a father who had discovered his son's true talent, Earl started playing golf with Tiger every day. It was a good diversion for the boy, and it also meant that father and son could spend some quality time together, bonding over a sport that they both loved. And it kept toddler Tiger occupied for hours.

TWO-YEAR-OLD TIGER WOODS had charisma to spare when he appeared on the *Mike Douglas Show* to putt a ball against Bob Hope. It was an iconic moment that almost didn't happen; Bob Hope's segment had gone a little long. Backstage, producers told Earl Woods that Tiger might be bumped from the show. After all, Douglas still had to interview Jimmy Stewart and child actress Kristy McNichol. There just might not be time for Tiger. But minutes before the end, Earl got the news that the schedule had worked itself out; the show would go on.

It was a cute segment: Tiger demonstrated his swing to Douglas, then putted against Bob Hope. The audience responded warmly and enthusiastically while Earl smiled contentedly. Tiger had the power to work the crowd.

The *Mike Douglas* appearance was a calculated move by Earl, who had been trying to get Tiger some national media coverage. Earl's year as an army spokesman had taught him the importance of the media; with the right media attention, Tiger could become famous. It would be the first time that Earl would use the media to further Tiger's career, a tactic that would eventually become a habitual pattern in their lives.

If Tiger was going to become a media darling, Earl thought, he needed to have the proper media training. Reporters were all alike; they wanted to get as much information as they could with as little effort as possible. When in the army, Earl had liked to make reporters work for their information; he had learned the fine art of answering only what they asked. If they needed more information, they could ask a follow-up question. He decided to teach Tiger the same thing.

"Tiger," Earl said to his son, "tell me, how old are you?"

"I'm three," Tiger responded. "I'll be four in December."

"That's not what I asked," Earl scolded with a smile. "I asked you how old you were, not when you'd have your next birthday. You should only answer what I ask you. Let's try that again. How old are you?"

"I'm three," Tiger answered, before pursing his lips tightly shut; he wasn't going to answer anything else.

"Good job," Earl complimented him. "What's your dog's name?"

"My dog's name is Toba," said Tiger, again pursing his lips tightly, as if trying to keep any more words from escaping.

"Excellent," said Earl. "But you don't have to shut your mouth so tightly after every question."

The restraint that Tiger needed with the media was equaled by his focus on the golf course; Tiger had become a disciplined, thoughtful boy who knew how to speak to adults on his own terms, not on theirs. His golf game was improving as well. In the fall of 1979, when he was still three years old, Tiger and Earl went to the Navy Gold Club about two miles from their house. Shooting nine holes, Tiger scored a 48—well over the par of 32, but extremely impressive for a toddler.

It wasn't long before news and entertainment shows began to take notice of the little boy from California who could hit the golf ball like a pro. Before he ever went to school, Tiger appeared as the subject of a short *Golf Digest* article. At five, he appeared on the ABC show *That's Incredible*. After the show, adults approached Tiger for an autograph. He didn't know how to sign his full name yet, but he could print "TIGER" in capital letters.

• • •

"DADDY, CAN WE SEND THIS to the kids?" Tiger's four-year-old voice startled Earl, who had been watching the console television. Earl looked at his son; he was holding a collection of gold coins. The coins were Tiger's pride and joy; he would often lie on his bed and stare at them.

Earl eyed Tiger with a mixture of amusement and puzzlement. "What kids?"

"Those kids right there," Tiger said, pointing at the television set.

Earl looked at the television. He had been watching a telethon to help feed starving children in Ethiopia. He looked back into his son's earnest eyes. "I see," he said slowly. "You want to give them your money?"

"Yes, Daddy," Tiger responded. "Can we send this to them?"

Earl looked away for a moment, partly to buy himself a few extra seconds to think and partly to blink back tears. He turned back to his pajama-clad son, surprised and overwhelmed by the boy's tender heart and generosity.

"Yes, I think we can send this to them," he said to Tiger, taking the coins. Later, he would figure out the cash equivalent—about $25—and send the money to a doctor he knew who was working in Ethiopia. Earl hid the coins, first under his bed, then later in a safety deposit box. When Tiger was an adult, Earl decided, he'd give the coins back. But for now, they would remain hidden. Two decades later, Earl would explain his decision to keep the coins. "I wanted him to understand that it was great to do good things for people, but that even good works can sometimes cost you," he said. "I could have told him, 'Son, keep your money,' and sent my own cash to the charity, but what would that teach him? That he didn't have to sacrifice? He needed to make the sacrifice himself."

There was little sacrifice in the Woods household, at least when it came to material possessions. Earl's pension, combined with the salary from his new job at McDonnell Douglas, gave them a comfortable middle-class existence. Their two-story, three-bedroom home sat on a corner lot in a neat neighborhood off a busy road in Cypress. Although the contemporary-style house was not opulent, it was big enough for a family of three. Earl often thought that his parents would have considered the Cypress home a castle, a mansion with more than enough living space. But Earl just called it home.

Not only did Tiger use the garage as his personal golf course, but he also often used the entire house as his putting green. Setting up obstacles for himself, he'd putt the ball around the common areas: under the coffee table, next to the fireplace, over the lamp. There was always golf equipment strewn around the house, at least until Kultida decreed that it was a cleanup day; then Tiger would put everything in its place.

Earl would later recall that Cypress was a racially homogeneous city where Tiger stood out as one of the only minority children. Earl was partially correct: Cypress had a small black community, with less than 5 percent of the population identifying themselves as African American. Still, Cypress was a surprisingly diverse city of nearly 50,000 residents, even during Tiger's childhood. According to census reports, more than 20 percent of the residents were Asian in 1980; another 12 percent were Hispanic. Even though Tiger may have felt that his was the sole dark face in a sea of whiteness, he was simply part of the gumbo of cultures in Southern California. No matter what the statistics said, however, Earl would maintain that one of Tiger's greatest obstacles was his race.

It was an exciting day for Tiger Woods, all dressed up for his first day of kindergarten on a sunny September morning in 1981. Kultida had scrubbed his five-year-old face and combed his hair, all the while telling him that he was going to love school. He'd get to play with all the other children, something he rarely got to do as an only child. With an expectant smile on his face, Tiger headed off to Cerritos Elementary School, ready for his newest adventure.

But the day ended in disaster when three white sixth-grade boys tied him to a tree, spray-painted the word "nigger" on him, and threw rocks at him. Tiger would talk about this incident in adulthood, remembering it as a moment of trauma that he said forever shaped the way he saw race relations. As with all Tiger Woods stories, however, the kindergarten incident was not without controversy or conflicting accounts. The school principal denied that the incident had ever happened, as did some of the teachers, but even though there was no proof either way, it became part of the public story of Tiger. Whatever happened in September 1981 would remain a mystery, but the aftereffects would resonate with Tiger into adulthood.

Numerous times during Tiger's childhood, Kultida sat down with him to discuss racism. He was just as good as everyone else, she told him, no less a person than any white child. She instructed him not to act out in hate or in retaliation for the treatment he received; he just needed to be strong and resist the temptation to retaliate. He could over-come anything that people said about him. It was a discussion that somewhat annoyed Kultida; she hadn't faced this kind of racism in Thailand, at least not as blatantly. It annoyed her that a country as advanced and seemingly open-minded as America could have such antiquated attitudes toward race.

By the first grade, Tiger had developed a severe stutter; it surfaced at the beginning of hard conso-nants and seemed to get worse if he was tired, angry, or scared. Tiger often took a long time to choke out a sentence, and he started getting teased for his speech impediment. Earl and Kultida took Tiger to speech therapists, but no matter what treatment they recommended, they were consistently unsuccessful in teaching Tiger how to speak smoothly. As the year progressed, Tiger slowly started to overcome the stutter, and by the end of the year it was gone. Each member of the family had a different theory of how he had conquered his stammer. Tiger would say he had practiced talking to the family dog, talking slowly and evenly until his jumbled words became smooth. Earl believed that Tiger had stopped stuttering when Kultida stopped speaking Thai to him at home. Kultida thought that Tiger had merely outgrown the speech problem.

SEVEN-YEAR-OLD TIGER WOODS lined up to putt at the Long Beach Navy Golf Course. The warm spring day was perfect: blue skies, comfortable temperatures, and the stillness that often accompanies a clear day on a golf course. As Tiger drew back his club to swing, the silence was pierced by a metallic clinking sound; Earl was jingling the change in his pockets.

"Dad," a visibly annoyed Tiger sighed, "stop it."

Earl looked at his son with a cheeky grin. "Stop what?"

"Stop making noise, Dad," Tiger responded. "I'm trying to concentrate."

"You can concentrate with me making noise." Earl's amusement continued to annoy Tiger, who lined up the putt again.

As Tiger swung the golf club, a loud staccato cough stabbed at the silence again. "Dad," Tiger complained, the tone of his voice rising to a whine, "quit doing that."

"Sorry, I had to cough," Earl replied with a grin. He was clearly enjoying his role as antagonist; it was a role that he took on quite easily. "It won't happen again."

And so it went. Every time Tiger swung the club, Earl made noise: talking, singing, dropping his golf bag. Tiger had two choices: to focus, block out the distraction, and make his shot, or to lose his composure and yell at his father. He alternated between the two.

"I wanted to teach him mental toughness," Earl would say in 2004. "Golf is mental; I wanted him to be mentally strong so he could concentrate, no matter what was going on. If he got distracted by the little things I did, he'd never be able to handle the pressure of a tournament. I know it was annoying, but it was really to teach him." He paused and then continued with a grin. "Plus, it was always fun to give him the business."

Did Earl ever go too far? Both he and Tiger would always say no, that Earl was just training a champion. He expected greatness, but acted out of love. Tiger and Earl would always maintain that

Tiger's training was fun, something he really enjoyed, perhaps even a bonding experience between father and son. But their assertions didn't always match reality. When Tiger was eleven, Earl started a six-month "boot camp" to teach Tiger mental toughness. "It was brutal," Earl would tell *People* magazine a decade later. "Prisoner-of-war interrogation techniques, psychological intimidation—it went on and on."

"Earl often got in Tiger's face," explained a golf writer who spent a lot of time with the Woodses in the early 1990s. "Just taunting him, saying horrible things to him. I know he wants everyone to think that it was a gentle time between himself and Tiger, like he would just be a cheerleader and encourager. Of course there was a lot of that, but there was a lot of bullying, also."

Twenty years later, Tiger would use various words to describe how Earl had made him feel during that period: "Frustrated" and "insignificant" were two of the most frequent words he used. It would have been grueling training for anyone, let alone a boy in his preteen years. After Tiger became the World's Best Golfer, Earl would say that Tiger had requested the training, had wanted the instruction and reveled in the discipline. Tiger would say that Earl knew where the line was and that he had never crossed it. When Tiger was an adult, the narrative was that Tiger always appreciated Earl's instruction, although Earl would sheep-

ishly admit that Tiger had occasionally shed stinging tears of frustration during the training sessions.

There was a lot of pressure on Tiger to succeed
at golf; Earl claimed that he tried not to ride him
or to make him feel that winning at golf was the
only way for him to be loved. In fact, Earl always
pulled Tiger aside on the course to reaffirm that
golf was just a game; it wouldn't affect how Earl
felt about him.

"Tiger, you can do something else today," Earl
would say. "You don't have to play golf."

"But I want to play golf, Daddy," Tiger would
respond.

"But don't you want to go play with your
friends?"

"No," Tiger would say. "I'd rather stay here with
you."

Earl was flattered that Tiger was so enamored
with him that they had become best friends; after
all, he hadn't had a close relationship with his
other sons. But Earl would later claim that he often
wondered whether Tiger pushed himself too hard
and took things more seriously than he needed to.

"He'd get so upset when he missed a putt," Earl
said in 2004. "Just so angry and furious at himself.
I always had to remind him that everything was
okay, that he was doing fine. He needed to know
that in the scheme of things, it was really not a
big deal."

Not everyone bought Earl's claims of his laid-back training. "That's revisionist history," explained the golf writer. "Earl was very tough on Tiger; whether he was too tough or not is debatable. But he wasn't always calm and he wasn't always kind. Sometimes, he could be a real jerk."

If Earl was the golf coach in the house, Kultida was everything else: disciplinarian, warden, cheerleader, and chauffeur. Earl was Tiger's friend, his easygoing golfing buddy who would be there to talk about anything. Kultida Woods was not her son's friend; she was his mother, a strong disciplinarian who made sure that homework was done, chores were completed, and respect was paid to elders. Disobedience and lying were crimes punishable by a spanking; Kultida truly believed that sparing the rod would, in fact, spoil the child. Earl didn't spank; he might lecture sometimes, but he left the corporal punishment to Kultida. He hated to spank Tiger; besides, who would want to listen to all that crying?

Tiger feared Kultida, not as an enemy, but as someone he respected. Kultida didn't put up with nonsense, at least not for very long; she expected Tiger to be well mannered and polite. There was only one punishment in the Woods household that was worse than a spanking: If Tiger was disrespectful or lazy, Kultida took away his golf clubs, a punishment that always ended in tears.

Tiger was nine years old when Kultida took him to Thailand to introduce him to her native country.

She brought him to a Buddhist monk to analyze a chart she had kept on Tiger's life. Unaware of Tiger's accomplishments on the golf course, the monk told Kultida that Tiger was a special child destined for leadership. If he went into the military, she was told, he would become a four-star general.

Tiger's decision to become a Buddhist was a choice he made as a child to follow the religion of his mother. Both Earl and Kultida had promised not to pressure him; he could choose his own religion. But Earl wasn't devout; he didn't practice Christianity in the same way that Kultida practiced Buddhism. She felt that it gave her an inner peace, a tranquility that helped her to cope with the chaos around her. It had been a stabilizing force in her life, and she was thrilled that Tiger was interested in following it as well.

When Tiger was young, he and Kultida would practice their Buddhism together. "Tiger and Kultida used to meditate every night in their living room as he was growing up," explained a family friend. "Kultida used Buddhism to give him some peace after a day on the course with his father. Earl would push him hard during the day, and Kultida would help center him at night through prayer and meditation."

Tiger continued his nightly meditation into adulthood, but he drifted away from some of the teachings that Kultida espoused. She believed that she could reach ultimate enlightenment through Buddhism. Tiger, however, believed that it was impossible to achieve perfection. The best he could do was strive to make himself into the best person he could possibly be.

Tiger would later credit his mother, not his father, with instilling in him a competitive drive and a killer instinct. When Earl was unavailable, it was Kultida—in bright patterns and cherry-red lipstick—who drove Tiger to his junior competitions. She didn't look the part of a cheerleader; she seldom cracked a smile as she followed him along the course. Kultida stood in the gallery, eyebrows knit into a preoccupied scowl, scrutinizing Tiger's every move. The corners of her mouth pinched downward, not in displeasure, but in deep contemplation. She was an analyst, gauging what her son did right and what he did wrong. In the car on the way home, Kultida would tell Tiger what she thought of his game; she wasn't the pro that Earl was, but she gave her feedback anyway.

Kultida had always been a fighter: grappling for her parents' attention, striving to get noticed in boarding school, toiling for recognition in a man's world. She purposefully and deliberately imparted her competitive drive to Tiger, not only in golf, but also in everything he did. Earl turned everything into a game; Kultida turned it into a competition. It wasn't enough for Tiger to succeed; his competition had to lose.

Tiger was only eight when he won in the

youngest age group available at the Junior World Golf Tournament. The competition was meant for nine- and ten-year-olds, but a special exemption allowed Tiger to participate. Ever the promoter, Earl turned the victory into another part of the Tiger Woods lore: He could compete, and win, against people much more experienced than he was.

Earl's work as an army spokesman had taught him the importance of buzz. The media liked a story with a strong narrative, an intriguing central character, and an emotional punch. The story of Tiger Woods had all three components; Earl just had to be sure to package it correctly. Earl calculatedly and shrewdly started building Tiger's brand before anyone even knew who he was.

Tiger's athleticism was not limited to golf. Earl would take Tiger to the park to throw around a baseball; it was another bonding experience for father and son to play a sport that was so important to Earl.

Injuries were common in the Woods household, with Tiger coming home with the requisite bumps and bruises of a preteen. When he was ten, Tiger's friends carried him back to the house. While running to catch a punt during a pickup football game in the park, Tiger had run into a tree, which knocked him unconscious. It wasn't that Tiger was clumsy or uncoordinated; it was just that he was so focused on the sport, so committed to winning, that he disregarded his personal safety.

"Tiger was his own best friend and worst enemy," Earl would later say. "He put a lot of pressure on himself, and he'd not know when to quit. He pushed himself really hard. But I admired it; I admired how he could hold onto something like a bulldog, never giving up."

Tiger was the center of Earl and Kultida's world; his golf career became the family's top priority. Every spare moment was focused on Tiger, and his parents soon found themselves drifting apart. Tiger always claimed not to have noticed anything different between his parents. Earl and Kultida weren't affectionate people; they had never been demonstrative in their love for each other.

Tiger's golf career cost the family financially, although Earl and Kultida took pains not to let Tiger know about the sacrifices they were making. Earl would later estimate that travel, equipment, and tournament entrance fees cost the family about $30,000 per year. What Earl and Kultida could not scrounge from Earl's $53,000 salary, they would secure by taking out home equity mortgages on their Cypress house. It was stressful to Kultida to see them unable to get ahead; she was unsure that they were making the right moves, sacrificing the family's well-being so that Tiger could play golf. Although she was stressed about the finances, Kultida decided not to make waves; Earl was the breadwinner, and she would leave the family's finances to him. Besides, she could see that golf was the only thing that gave Tiger real confidence. It was more than a hobby for him; it was his way of dealing with adolescence. He had some trouble adjusting socially, and golf seemed to be a good outlet.

THEY WERE COKE-BOTTLE GLASSES, the kind of eyewear that could get a kid teased, if not beaten up; they distorted his eyes and made him an easy target for jokes and ridicule. Tiger was severely nearsighted. Throughout elementary school, he started noticing things getting blurrier: the chalkboard, his friends' faces, and, most troublingly, golf balls. Earl and Kultida took him to an optometrist and had him fitted with glasses.

The eyewear just completed the look that Tiger would sport throughout junior high: the thick, unruly hair that stuck out in all the wrong places; the bargain-brand clothes that just didn't fit right; and the unfortunate habit of looking downward when he spoke. To Tiger, this awkward junior high phase seemed to last forever. He was so used to everything being wrong and to knowing that he would never be prom king or the star quarterback on the football team. All he could be was a golf star, which did nothing for his social standing.

"Tiger didn't make any waves," says junior high classmate Tammy Reeder. "He was always there on the side, with a silly smile on his face. It was like he was hoping to be included, but I think he was ignored a lot. After he became famous, everyone came forward and talked about how they were such good friends of Tiger's, and it was ridiculous. Those were the people who didn't give him the time of day in school."

Tiger was not one of the cool kids; he didn't get much attention from girls, and some boys found it easier to ignore him when they weren't making cracks behind his back. Tiger had his friends, but they were from the same social stratum: kids who seldom stood a chance of moving up the social ladder. No one really disliked Tiger; he just wasn't part of the junior high power structure.

Tiger had always had a few friends. Usually, they were other kids who languished in the middle third of the high school pecking order, neither the gods nor the pariahs. He wasn't the type to be shoved into lockers by bullies—they would have had to notice him to bully him—but he wasn't doing the bullying, either. He was a nonentity, a kid always on the periphery of his peers' social circles, a bystander in their social interactions. As a result, he was hardly remembered by his classmates from elementary and junior high; he just didn't stand out.

Tiger understood that he probably wasn't going to get the acceptance of his peers; the junior high caste system is rigid, and it's rare that students can really move up the ladder. He spent some time worrying about this, but ultimately decided to focus his preteen angst on golf.

Tiger was eleven years old when he beat Earl Woods at golf the first time, shooting a 71 to best his father's score by a stroke at the Long Beach Navy Golf Course. Earl credited the loss with a change in his outlook: He no longer cared about beating his son at golf; from that moment on, it was all about Tiger's score.

Earl wasn't the only one to see the progress in Tiger's game. Tiger went on to win the Junior World Championships six times, including four consecutive wins from 1988 to 1991. Tiger Woods was already a force, a prodigy who left his competitors in the dust. Even adults weren't immune to losing against Tiger Woods; he was better than most people who had been playing the sport for decades. And he wasn't even in high school yet.

CHAPTER 5

IT WAS A SUBTLE FLIRTATION, nearly impercep-
tible to the people around them. If anyone had been
paying attention, they would have noticed that
Tiger Woods was eyeing the leggy blonde sitting
next to him in the two-story Western High School
library in Anaheim, California. It was April 1992,
just days before riots in Los Angeles would change
the face of race relations in Southern California,
and the region was collectively holding its breath
to hear the verdict in the Rodney King case.
Despite the bubbling racial tensions in the area,
few students at Western High gave a second
thought to interracial dating. The student body was
diverse, and students of different races were always
hooking up. There may have been comments made
here and there, but no one said anything to Tiger.

Tiger had wanted to shed his nerdy image before
enrolling in high school, and for the most part he
succeeded in updating his look. The glasses were
replaced with contact lenses. He had his thick curls
cut shorter so that they wouldn't be as unruly. He
even bought some new clothes to update his style.
The style renovation worked, and Tiger managed
to do what so many high school students wish they
could achieve: put some of his awkwardness
behind him and create a new persona. Whatever his
insecurities were, they were not evident from his

outward appearance. There was no longer anything wrong with him, at least not physically.

Tiger had started to sprout up. He had never really stood out, but now he was getting close to six feet tall; his body had gotten leaner as it shed baby fat. He was turning into a handsome guy, someone the girls would notice if they had not previously known about his awkward junior high years.

His extreme makeover did the job that Tiger had intended it to do. He started to receive a little more attention, mostly from girls who liked his unassuming and soft-spoken demeanor. Earl and Kultida had taught him the importance of being unfailingly polite; he was a gentleman who spoke to girls with respect.

Although his politeness served him well after graduation, it was not a valued commodity in high school. No matter what he did, Tiger would never fit into the prom king mold, but he did manage to attain some level of acceptance from his peers. He was a nice guy, a kid generally liked by his peers in a nebulous, arm's-length way.

He might have lost the coke-bottle glasses, but Tiger was still painfully shy, and he still had the habit of looking down when he spoke to his classmates and teachers. Other students would describe him as quiet and reserved, but the truth was that Tiger was intimidated by the other students, and the only place he felt truly comfortable was on the golf course. He had considerable poise but not a lot of charisma, at least not yet. That would come later.

Despite the changes between junior high and high school, Tiger's commitment to golf remained as fierce and unwavering as always. Now he was more than a little boy who could hit a golf ball hard; he was a young man who had a venue in which to compete. By the time he was fourteen, Tiger had learned how to schedule all the travel for his golf tournaments; he was becoming a competent man. It was all part of Earl and Kultida's agenda; he would know how to handle himself.

The tournaments would compare his skills with those of other kids his age; instead of being an oddity, he could become a champion. In 1991, he won the U.S. Junior Amateur Championship; he was the youngest winner ever at fifteen years, six months old. At the end of the year, *Golf Digest* named him the Junior Amateur Player of the year, an honor that he got on his sixteenth birthday. The media started generating buzz about the wunderkind from Cypress, a golfer who was so good that he had the potential to become the best golfer in history. It didn't really make much difference to Tiger what the media were saying about him; he wasn't in competitive golf for the attention. Besides, he hated talking to reporters.

WITH A YELLOW WALKMAN attached to his belt and headphones in his ears, Tiger looked every bit the typical sixteen-year-old he was when he gave his first interview to *People* magazine. The editors of the magazine thought he was young, charismatic, and groundbreaking, a good fit for a one-page story.

Tom Cunneff, then a staff writer for the celebrity weekly, went to Michigan to meet Tiger on a golf course as he practiced. Cunneff watched Tiger putt a few balls, all the while listening to Earl Woods talk about his son in glowing superlatives. Tiger wasn't very chatty—he just didn't have a lot to say—but Earl compensated for his son's reticence by talking openly about Tiger's background and golf training. Tiger might have been tight-lipped, but Earl was a blabbermouth in the best sense of the word: one who followed up each of his anecdotes with a pithy quote.

Everything Earl said was a good sound bite. It was hard to tell whether this was involuntary or purposeful. It seemed as though Earl had conditioned himself to punctuate his stories with short, staccato sentences that could fit perfectly into a photo caption. He could paint a picture of Tiger with words and knew how to compensate for Tiger's introversion.

Even at sixteen, Tiger was something of an enigma, at least as far as the media were concerned. His father's training and exposure to the press made Tiger a focused, seasoned professional at dealing with reporters; he had long ago determined that he didn't enjoy giving interviews. He was never surly or unprofessional, but his one-word answers made him seem unwilling or unable to really open up to reporters, to tell them how he was really feeling. Even in his mid-teens, Tiger had learned the fine art of the platitude: using clichés and tired expressions to answer questions rather than giving reporters any insight into his world. With Tiger, it was hard to get him to say sentences that started with "I." Instead, he would offer up generalities, dispensing proverbs and Confucianisms as substitutes for substance.

"I want to be the Michael Jordan of golf," Tiger told Tom Cunneff. It was something he had said countless times before to dozens of interviewers in the previous weeks. The repetition of sound bites was a habit that would follow Tiger throughout his career; he would choose a statement and repeat it over and over to reporters. It was as if he chose certain innocuous statements to disseminate to everyone in the media, a verbal equivalent of a press release. No one got the exclusive, and no one would be able to pierce Tiger's armor.

Tiger and Tom spoke for an hour in 1994. Tom asked probing questions of Tiger in the hopes of getting something profound, a deeper under-standing of what made Tiger tick. Tiger continued to give shallow answers. He wasn't being rude; he was just a sixteen-year-old with little to say. The interview continued without much change in Tiger's demeanor until Tom touched on the topic of the prejudice that Tiger had faced when he was younger. "He perked right up," Tom recalls. "He finally had something to say."

Tiger had never been barred from playing at clubs; in the 1980s and 1990s, people were too savvy to participate in such blatant racism. Instead, there was a general feeling of unwelcome that followed Tiger when he hit the links; he was an oddity, and not one that was necessarily appreciated or embraced. People would stare at Tiger in the clubhouse, not even trying to hide their gawking. It was as if they were silently wondering, "What is that kid doing here?"

Tiger told Cunneff that he had developed a foolproof way to counter the stares, to turn the tables. "I would just stare back," he said. "When people look at you, and you turn around and look at them, they always look away."

It was a passionate subject for the young Tiger; life had given him an insight about racial issues that not everyone had. He seemed preoccupied with the realization that his race kept him from really fitting in with other golfers; he would always be different, no matter how well he played. In many ways, it seemed that the golf community would be just like high school, and he'd never be the prom king.

"Prejudice definitely rubbed him the wrong way," says Cunneff. "It certainly drove him in some respects. It really bothered him. It was the one thing he was passionate about; when we talked about other things, he had the tone of 'whatever,' but when we talked about this, I could feel his emotion. I could detect his anger about it."

Although Tiger may have been unwelcome to some of the white club members, he quickly developed a following of African Americans, mostly middle-aged men, who watched in awe as he hit the ball. There was a pride about Tiger Woods; he had already accomplished a lot as a sixteen-year-old, and his new fans wanted to see where he'd end up. Tiger was a source of racial pride among African Americans, many of whom knew his name long before the rest of the world had any idea who he was.

As Tiger finished his interview with Tom Cunneff, Earl had to go somewhere; he was always disappearing while Tiger was playing golf, and no one really knew where he went. "He left the interview early," says Cunneff, "probably to do what we all know now to be true." Earl asked him to give Tiger a ride back to the hotel, a favor that Cunneff was happy to grant.

During the silent drive, Tom searched for something to say to Tiger, a bit of wisdom that he, as a seasoned journalist, could impart to such a young kid. "He was pretty jaded," Cunneff remembers. "This was nothing new to him. I said to him, 'When you turn pro, please try not to use clichés, because so many athletes use clichés. Try to answer the questions and talk from the heart.' Tiger just looked at me like I was crazy; he had heard it all before."

Tiger's relationship with the media would always be an annoyance to him, a thorn in his side. At first, he may have resisted the press because he had nothing to say, but he would eventually come to resent the press for asking questions he didn't want to answer. It's hard to say how, or if, his attitude toward the media evolved over the years; he was always too taciturn to reveal his true feelings about the matter. Despite his disdain, the media attention was here to stay; he was too interesting and talented to ignore.

The more Tiger played golf, the more media attention he received and the more accolades came his way. In February 1992, the sixteen-year-old played in the Nissan Los Angeles Open at Riviera Country Club in Pacific Palisades. (It would be the site of his first PGA Tour event as an amateur player.) If there had been any doubt that he would eventually go pro, all doubts were erased by his stellar year in 1992, during which he won five amateur titles. He won the U.S. Junior Amateur Championship for a second time in July, the only golfer to win twice. *Golf World* and *Golf Digest* named him their Player of the Year, and *Golfweek* named him the National Amateur of the Year. At sixteen, he was the most promising athlete in the sport.

TIGER WAS NOT A LADIES' MAN, at least not in the strictest sense of the term. He had overcome his junior high nerdiness to become reasonably popular in the 2,000-student school—he would eventually be chosen most likely to succeed—and he enjoyed a nice-guy persona that both helped and hurt him with members of the opposite sex. Tiger wasn't named the class flirt or the most handsome or any other superlatives that usually connote sex appeal. He was a good guy who worked hard and got good grades. He was best friend material to many girls, but they never saw him as a possible romantic suitor; he lacked the bad boy image that often attracts teenage girls. This lack of game bothered Tiger; he desperately wanted a girlfriend but instead found himself relegated to the role of best friend, the shoulder for pretty girls to cry on when the other boys broke their hearts.

But Tiger's luck with women began to change during his junior year. Tiger was coyly smiling at his first real girlfriend: Dina Gravell, a cheerleader with flawless skin and a perfect California tan. Dina raised Tiger's profile around the school, and he relished the extra attention that he was now receiving from classmates, especially girls. Tiger had suddenly realized a life lesson: Women would be more interested in him if he was dating someone else, especially if that woman was a pretty, popular, petite blonde like Dina. Tiger told friends that he wasn't going to mess up this relationship; it was too important to him.

Tiger had been determined to make his move

from the moment he saw Dina in his accounting class, but his overwhelming shyness made dating a challenge. He took weeks to muster the courage to ask her to the movies; when he finally did, it was more of a stammered suggestion than an actual proposal. Dina wasn't just a girl; she was the embodiment of everything Tiger wanted: a sexy, blonde, popular cheerleader. She had the power to make him feel awkward, to render him speechless about mundane topics. After their first date, he leaned in for an awkward kiss that instead became a hug.

Dina was the Mercedes of high school girls, and Tiger fell for her quickly. His feelings weren't exactly love; they were a mixture of appreciation and infatuation. Tiger seemed to care more about the concept of having a girlfriend than he cared about Dina, at least at the beginning of their adolescent relationship. As the couple stayed together, however, Tiger started developing clear feelings for her. During classes, he sent her increasingly amorous notes; she responded in kind. Suddenly, Tiger Woods had a steady, exclusive girlfriend. Whether or not he was in love, he didn't know. But he knew that he wanted to be around her all the time, and she felt the same way about him.

Earl and Kultida Woods liked Dina, at least as much as they could like any girl who would distract Tiger from both his studies and his amateur golf career. Earl realized that a pretty girl could quickly undo all the hard work that he had poured into

Tiger, and he felt slightly threatened by Dina. But what could he do? If he showed any disapproval of Dina, Tiger would be more resolved to date her—perhaps rebelling against his training. Instead, Earl chose to embrace Dina, welcoming her as part of the family. She was a common fixture around the Woods home, often staying for dinner or hanging out with Tiger in the living room. It was a casual, comfortable, high school relationship.

He wasn't a rebellious kid, at least not as far as Earl and Kultida were concerned. He had picked up an interest in rap and hip-hop music; the beat and the lyrics set Earl's teeth on edge, but he could live with both. In many ways, Tiger was a stereotypical teen, a fan of professional wrestling and *The Simpsons*. But Tiger was a respectful son, a product of his parents' instruction, and they had few real complaints about his behavior.

As Tiger continued through high school, his bond with Earl deepened. Although Tiger was close with Kultida, it was Earl who now took him to most of the tournaments; the hours spent in the car were bonding times for father and son.

Despite the family closeness, there were cracks in the veneer. Earl and Kultida's marriage wasn't as strong as it appeared; the years of focusing on Tiger had caused them to drift apart, and their lives became separate and distant. Kultida busied herself with domestic chores, making sure the house was clean, the food was cooked, and Tiger was content. Earl immersed himself in Tiger's career, training him and talking him up to anyone who would listen. Earl and Kultida didn't dislike each other; they usually spoke to each other in reserved, respectful tones. Their conversations were often superficial: discussions over the logistics of who would take Tiger to his next tournament or how they were going to afford the next plane ticket. As Tiger got older, his parents just weren't as close as they had once been, and it seemed unlikely that they'd ever recapture that intimacy.

But Earl had another proclivity, something that golf writers had whispered about for years but chose not to divulge. When Earl took Tiger to junior tournaments, they often left Kultida back home in Cypress. Money was tight, and it was often impossible to buy three plane tickets when only two were necessary. Once apart from his wife, Earl turned on the charm with women—some of whom were fans of his son. "Earl would be out with different women at Tiger's tournaments," says a golf writer who met Tiger as a teen. "While Tiger would play a round, Earl would play around."

It was an open secret, at least in certain golf circles. Earl had a roving eye and an interest in the ladies. He would often disappear from the tournaments for hours at a time, often to Tiger's annoyance. "Tiger was often mad at his dad for his philandering," says the writer. "He hated it."

Years later, when Tiger would himself become

embroiled in scandal, Dina Gravell would come forward and allege in the media that Tiger had tearfully called her to report that Earl was cheating with women. Her allegation would fit into a narrative that defined the relationship between Earl and Tiger: Tiger idolized his father and tried to emulate him. He picked up many of Earl's positive traits—his discipline and focus—but also some of the bad ones.

Although Earl's proclivities were known in the golf world, many writers eschewed any mention of it. "It wasn't relevant before," says Tom Cunneff, who went on to become a senior editor for *Links* magazine. "Nobody really cared what his dad did. Obviously, people do now. But they didn't care back then.

"Nobody would have gone near that before," says Cunneff. "Golf writers wouldn't go near it, because they needed access to him. It's more important to get Tiger to give you a couple of quotes after his round than to write about some rumor you've heard."

It was the beginning of Tiger's uncanny knack for manipulating and controlling his press. Reporters wanted to have access to Tiger, to be close to him. They wouldn't dare jeopardize that closeness by reporting anything scandalous.

By the time Tiger won the U.S. Junior Amateur Championship for a record third time in July 1993, it was clear that he was going to be around for a long time; the media would have to be good to him. Besides, there really wasn't anything negative to say.

TIGER HAD ALWAYS BEEN a good student, but he flourished in high school, becoming a member of the National Honor Society, taking advanced placement classes, and maintaining a 3.98 GPA. He actually liked academics; he was always prepared for class, and he participated in discussions. He had nearly perfect attendance—the only days he missed were unavoidable conflicts with his golf tournaments.

Tiger's academic success occurred in spite of Earl Woods, who often didn't think education was as important as golf. Earl did pay lip service to education; he was smart enough to realize the importance of appearing to support Tiger's academics, not only to appease public perception, but also to keep the peace with Kultida. Tiger could make a lot of money in golf, surely more than most people would ever earn from their day jobs; why study subjects he was not going to use? Kultida Woods, however, continued to insist that Tiger apply himself to his education. She policed Tiger, checking to see if his homework was done, making sure he studied for tests and quizzes. She would threaten to bar him from his next golf tournament if he didn't devote the necessary time to his schoolwork.

Her efforts created a studious boy who actually

valued the importance of learning. At age thirteen, Tiger had written a note to Stanford's golf coach at the time, Wally Goodwin. In the note, Tiger explained to Goodwin that he wanted to obtain a "quality business education." It was the type of pre-science that would define Tiger; he was constantly looking ahead, constantly planning his next step. In life, as on the golf course, Tiger was always several steps ahead, looking forward to the next success.

The letter impressed Goodwin, and he held onto it, showing it to the Stanford golfers each year. Tiger's ambition and drive were legendary, and Goodwin had written proof.

In 1994, Tiger made the decision to enroll in Stanford, and he began business classes in the fall. It would be the next step of his promising career. The relationship between Dina and Tiger continued to progress, and it took on the urgency of a typical teenage romance that would soon be undone by college. They continued to see each other almost every day, with passionate makeout sessions on their living room couches. There were petty fights and adolescent angst, but the relationship was a solid one. Tiger and Dina became inseparable, both at school and at home. She was a year ahead of him in school; when she graduated, she stayed in the area. They continued to grow serious as Tiger approached his 1994 graduation, and the relationship stayed intact when he went off to college at Stanford, four hundred miles away from home.

CHAPTER 6

IN THE END, there was never really any doubt about where Tiger would go to college. He wanted Stanford; Stanford wanted him. When he officially decided to attend, no one seemed very surprised; it just seemed inevitable. There were a lot of good things about Stanford. For one thing, it was consistently rated in the top ten schools for undergraduates. Geography had kept it from being part of the Ivy League, but Stanford was just as selective and prestigious. Besides, unlike the Ivy League schools, Stanford offered athletic scholarships.

He'd move out of the house in Cypress, of course: Stanford was an hour flight away from home. He was ready to go out on his own, to become a college man. He promised Kultida that he wouldn't go wild; he was in college to study and learn, not to party. He would make the most of the college experience.

Just two weeks before registering for his freshman classes at Stanford, Tiger had dazzled the golfing world with an incredible come-from-behind win at the U.S. Amateur golf tournament. He had been down by six strokes at the beginning of the final round, a deficit that would have been insurmountable for anyone but Tiger. Eighteen holes later, he had won by two strokes to become the U.S. Amateur's youngest winner ever.

It wasn't just the record amateur win that set Tiger apart; it was his jaw-dropping style, a combination of calculated gambling and competence. He was a showman on the course, a charismatic young man who had an indescribable magnetism that riveted the national television audience. Tiger had owned the TPC-Sawgrass course in Ponta Vedra Beach, Florida, at least during the final round, and it was clear to everyone that they were witnessing something special. As he sank the last putt, he collapsed tearfully into his father's arms, the first of many times he would do that after winning a tournament.

At eighteen, he had the golf world on a string. It was a heady, exciting time for Tiger, who had always acted older than his years. He was an adult now. Perhaps he wasn't as idealistic as his colleagues; he'd experienced too much to be as innocent as they were. But college sounded very appealing to him, and his youthful exuberance pumped him up for the next adventure.

Most coeds weren't aware of Tiger; they didn't follow golf and were therefore unimpressed with his achievements. To them, he was now just another freshman bringing his stuff onto campus, registering for classes, and figuring out how to find the library. Tiger didn't see his anonymity as a bad thing; he'd be able to blend in with the other students, enjoying a traditional college experience while playing on the golf team. He chose economics as his major; as he repeated to reporters, he wanted to manage the people who would eventually manage his money. He had a definite plan for his career: He would stay in college for all four years, finishing his bachelor's degree before moving on. Then he would go pro, but not until he had finished school. Getting his degree was a given, something he would do at all costs.

During his freshman year, Tiger was again interviewed by Tom Cunneff with *People* magazine for a feature article about his golf career. The previous two years had matured Tiger, and he spoke as a college man rather than a high school boy. "He talked about staying in school for all four years because he wanted to get a degree," remembers Cunneff. "He said, 'The priorities in my life have always been family first, school second, and golf third.' It seemed strange. You don't hear many 18-year-olds talk like that; people don't say that until they have kids of their own. It just seemed so programmed to me."

Perhaps the programmers were Earl and Kultida Woods. Both of them had encouraged Tiger to go to college, to further his education at one of the best schools in the country. After the U.S. Amateur, Earl had told reporters that Tiger was going to succeed in school. "My guidance to him was, you will get a degree," Earl said proudly. "With the emphasis on will. I was a baseball player in college, and no sports miss more school than baseball and golf. I told him, 'I made it in four years, and I'm a lot dumber than you.'"

A decade later, Earl would continue to extol the virtues of education. "Part of the reason why I wanted Tiger to go to college is that he's a role model," he explained. "If he didn't go to college, what type of message would that send? Maybe he didn't need to go to college in his particular case, but he had a responsibility to go for his fans. He had an example to set."

The edict had been issued, and Tiger knew what was expected of him. No matter what other opportunities came his way, no matter how many millions were offered to him, he was going to stay at Stanford until he graduated in 1998. This was nonnegotiable. After all, he was a role model.

To say that Tiger's profile was raised after the U.S. Amateur tournament would be an understatement. After his win, he received engraved invitations to compete in the big three: the U.S. Open, the British Open, and the Masters. But Tiger couldn't focus on such invitations; he had collegiate golf to play.

The semester was less than two weeks old when Tiger stepped up to the first tee as a collegian at the William H. Tucker Invitational at the University of New Mexico. He had an air of confidence that was rare for a freshman; he almost swaggered along the golf course. Nothing gave Tiger as much confidence as a golf tournament; it was the one place where he really stood out. Tiger was on his game; his swing was strong, and his mental game was precise. He shot a 68 in the first round, four under par. His team was thrilled; Tiger was going to have an amazing college career.

HAVING A GIRLFRIEND out of his league proved to be a problem for Tiger. His insecurities blossomed now that he was apart from Dina. Whom was she talking to? Did she have another boyfriend? Tiger couldn't know for sure. Tiger would have said that he trusted Dina; he didn't really think that she'd run off with someone else. But insecurity often leads to distrust, especially when there's a beautiful blonde at stake.

College was harder for Tiger than he had expected. His golf team generally liked him, but team members soon gave him an unfortunate nickname: Urkel, after the nerdy character on the popular TV show *Family Matters*. The character Urkel had no appeal with women and was constantly stymied as he pursued the woman of his dreams. Tiger hated the nickname and all it connoted, but he shrugged and laughed it off among his teammates; acceptance was the only way he could deal with it. But this silly nickname left Tiger with some serious concerns: Was this how his classmates saw him? Was this how women saw him? There were no easy answers, so Tiger stifled his worries and focused on his golf.

Tiger was busy, with a more hectic schedule than he had ever had before. His preoccupation with golf and academics started to strain his relationship with Dina. The love letters, which had previously been so frequent, started dwindling. He became less attentive when he came home on break, often waiting a few days before seeing her, and when he did, he'd demand to know if she had another boyfriend. Their relationship, once so casual and comfortable, had become dutiful and dull.

Earl saw this as an opportunity to rid Tiger of a distraction. He sat Tiger down and had a conversation about Dina. Was she really the love of his life? If there was no future in this relationship, Earl said, Tiger owed it to himself, and to Dina, to cut it off now. Besides, Earl asked, could they be sure that Dina wasn't interested in him for the money he would earn? No, it was best to end this relationship sooner rather than later. Tiger sent Dina a breakup letter; he never spoke to her again. There would be other women—pretty, leggy bombshells who would be interested in Tiger. He preferred blondes.

TIGER INSISTED THAT he had never considered the social significance of playing at Shoal Creek. As far as he was concerned, it was just another college tournament, one that he was determined to win. He wasn't there to make a social statement or to break down barriers; he was there to play golf.

And that was the crux of Tiger's annoyance with

the media during this era of his career. Everything had to mean something, at least to the reporters. Each decision he made was put into a larger context, and the media would speculate on the significance of everything, even the most mundane decisions. The media always made a big deal if he was the first African American to play somewhere or the youngest winner or whatever other superlative they could come up with at the time. The recognition was nice; it really was. But Tiger wasn't always striving to be the first or the youngest or even the greatest. He just wanted to win at golf.

But the media followed him at Shoal Creek like a pack of hunting dogs on point, because they all wanted his opinion on the rocky racial history of the course. Just four years earlier, Shoal Creek founder Hall Thompson had ignited a nationwide debate when he declared that his all-white club wouldn't be pressured into admitting African Americans before the PGA Championship was to be played there. Although the club had admitted one African American, the controversy had been unyielding, forcing the PGA to reevaluate the membership policies of clubs that hosted tournaments.

On this crisp October morning in 1994, the racial issue was still in the forefront of everyone's minds, from the activists protesting at the front gate to Thompson, who made a point of trailing after Tiger and enthusiastically complimenting his game. "I'm proud of you," he gushed to Tiger. "You're a great player." More than one hundred spectators followed Tiger, loudly clapping after every shot. It was the first time that Tiger had ever played on the Jack Nicklaus–designed course, and he might have enjoyed it more if everyone wasn't attaching a profound significance to the tournament. After Stanford emerged victorious, Tiger spoke to a handful of reporters who were far more interested in talking about race than golf.

Tiger had never wanted to become the poster boy for race relations in golf; he just wanted to hit the ball, to experience the course, and to play the game. Even though he still stung from the discrimination he had felt over the years, he didn't feel the necessity to always be the one to sound off on issues of race. Tiger didn't want to be part of a circus; he wanted to be seen as a player, not as an exhibit. He hoped that everyone could get over this obsession with his race; everything didn't have to be a profound message. Sometimes, it was all about the golf.

HE WAS RETURNING from dinner, slowly sauntering along the silent campus toward his dorm room. It was the evening of November 30, and Tiger didn't have any particular place to be; he had the unhurried gait of a college student with a dull Wednesday night ahead of him. It wasn't especially dark; the lights illuminated the parking lot, and Tiger didn't feel at all unsafe. He had walked this route many times—every day, in fact—and never had any problems.

He wasn't exactly sure where the man came from. He was dressed in dark clothes and carrying a large knife. He held it to Tiger's throat and demanded valuables. Tiger didn't have much cash on him, so the assailant snatched his watch and the gold chain around his neck. As he started to run away, the mugger turned and struck Tiger with the handle of the knife. It was a hard blow that cut Tiger's lip and knocked him to the ground. After the assailant ran away, a shaken Tiger hurried into the dorm and called Earl at home in Cypress. "Hey, Dad," Tiger started, shakily. "You know that over-bite I've always had? It's gone now." His ability to joke through the experience put Earl and Kultida's mind at ease; Tiger might have been mugged, but his sense of humor was intact. He was shaken, of course, but there would be no lasting damage.

College muggings don't normally make national news; they happen all the time on campuses around the country. But this was Tiger Woods, the young man who was predestined to change the world, and the story got wide national coverage. Even the *New York Times,* a continent away from Stanford, ran a seventy-two-word story about the incident. It was indicative of the media attention that surrounded the eighteen-year-old Tiger:

Anything that happened to Tiger, no matter how commonplace, was breaking news.

Despite the mugging, Tiger was enjoying his first taste of freedom. In many ways, he was the typical college student, an adult on his own for the first time. He hung out with his friends in the dorm and flirted with the pretty girls in his class. He wasn't a party animal. He didn't even drink very much, but he made a point of attending any parties he could; not only did they help him fit in, but he also could meet girls there, pretty girls who knew nothing about his gawky background. The high school awkwardness was gone; he was a college guy now, a man growing comfortable in his own skin, developing the cocky swagger of a college athlete.

During his freshman year, Tiger roomed with Notah Begay III, a student three years older than he was. Notah, an American Indian of Navajo and Pueblo descent, was the only other minority on the golf team. Through their shared experiences of being outsiders, Tiger and Notah became close friends. They hung out together, creating a circle of friends that would become an easy, comfortable clique.

Tiger and Notah loved crashing parties, especially the wild ones held at fraternity and sorority houses. They didn't have to be invited; they could just show up and not be turned away. One Saturday night, the two golfers heard about a party at the Sigma Chi frat house. Hoping to hook up with some cute girls, they developed a plan: They would hang out in the corner and survey the entire room for available girls to dance with. When they arrived, the party was packed, making it impossible for them to get a good view of everyone. Tiger wordlessly pointed at the five-foot-tall speakers being used by the DJ and climbed on top of one, while Notah clambered up another speaker. While the heavy bass pulsed, Tiger turned his back to the crowd and started shaking his butt. Before they knew it, Tiger and Notah were surrounded by pretty girls willing to dance with them.

"Tiger was really coming into his own," says a college friend. "He started off the first semester really shy, really reserved. But I think at some point, he said to himself, 'What the hell! I'm in college,' and really let himself have a good time.

"Tiger was naturally smart," says the friend. "So he didn't really have to study very much. He didn't spend his days in the library; he spent them hanging out. But his grades weren't half bad. He was the type who would come into class and say he hadn't studied for that day's exam, and he'd end up with a B-plus."

In addition to the frat parties, Tiger spent weekends at the gym or on the golf course with Notah. They became inseparable, developing an easy rapport of playful banter and friendly trash talk.

"They were just normal, down-to-earth college

guys," remembers Irene Folstrom, a prelaw student who briefly dated both Tiger and Notah. "Tiger was like a kid. He was a little boy at heart, who liked video games and McDonald's; he was just an all-American guy. He was a real gentleman. He knew how to treat girls and didn't seem the least bit creepy. He was just a really nice guy."

PLAYING THE MASTERS had always been a dream of Tiger's, a fantasy that he would indulge in from the time he was very young. Now, in April 1995, his dream of playing the course at Augusta National was about to come true. His win at the U.S. Amateur Championship had earned him the honor of appearing at the Masters. Tiger had shot a 72 for each of his first two rounds, which was enough to make the cut. By the end of the final round, he had tied for forty-first place with five over par, a respectable showing for a golfer who had not yet turned pro.

Tiger returned to Stanford feeling on top of the world until he got news that would quickly bring him back down to earth: He was in violation of NCAA rules because he had written diaries of his Masters experience for two weekly golf publications. Although he had received no compensation, he had not gotten the project approved. It was a minor, inadvertent violation, he was told. He would be suspended for only one day.

The punishment was little more than a slap on

the wrist, more of a symbolic gesture than anything else. Still, Tiger felt insulted by the castigation, because he didn't believe he had done anything wrong. But he was pragmatic enough to realize that anger would do him no good, and he let the matter drop, at least publicly.

But something had changed that day. Tiger was no longer enamored with playing college golf. Even though he still enjoyed it, he wondered whether he had transcended the NCAA rules; maybe he should go pro. His problem wasn't with Stanford; it was the NCAA that was making his life miserable, with rules that Tiger thought were arbitrarily enforced. Dropping out of school was certainly something to think about.

IT WAS GASTROENTERITIS, and Tiger had been throwing up all night. He was miserable, nauseous, and dehydrated, but if he stopped playing, Stanford would have to withdraw from the NCAA Men's West Regional golf tournament in Albuquerque. The team was already down a man—Casey Martin had also been hit by the illness—and if Tiger couldn't finish the round, Stanford would forfeit because it wouldn't have the required minimum of four players. Tiger's eyes were watery, and his body ached from retching all night. Between shots, he would lie down, hoping to somehow regain enough strength to continue.

It was another example of how deep Tiger was

able to dig; he had reserves of strength that even he didn't realize. In between the cramps that doubled him over in pain, Tiger somehow managed to shoot five birdies to score a 72 on the 7,300-yard championship course. Immediately after finishing the round, he was rushed to nearby University Hospital to be treated.

Tiger knew he had the fortitude to succeed in the mental game of golf; he had been trained for moments like this. But now he was becoming a star of the sports pages, an athlete who showed remarkable grit and determination. Publicly, he continued to reaffirm his commitment to finishing his degree, to giving three more years to Stanford before going pro. Tiger would say that he liked to finish what he started. But inwardly, the one-day suspension still lingered in the back of his mind. He could move past it, but he wouldn't forget how the suspension made him feel.

He played the U.S. Amateur Championship again in August and won the tournament by two strokes. It was his second consecutive win. It was clear that he had what it took to go pro, but the timing just wasn't right yet.

One thing Tiger wasn't looking forward to was the continual attention he would receive when he went pro. Already, he was starting to lose his anonymity, even on the Stanford campus. "Throngs of people would follow us wherever we went," says his college girlfriend Irene Folstrom.

"He didn't like it at all, and I didn't understand why he had become so popular."

Irene and Tiger spent a lot of time together on campus, writing their term papers together. "It was an amazing relationship," Irene remembers. "He was incredibly loyal to me, and I was to him. He never cheated on me. Never."

TIGER WASN'T GOING to turn down dinner with Arnold Palmer; he had always been a fan. When Tiger learned that Palmer would be at Napa, California, for a Senior PGA Tour event, he invited the older golfer to dinner. He wanted to seek some career advice from the golfer he most admired. It never crossed anyone's mind that the dinner could be controversial. Arnold wanted to share his wisdom with Tiger, and Tiger wanted to be in the company of his idol. They ate dinner in Napa Valley, having an hour-long conversation about the sport, Tiger's college career, and his plans to eventually go pro. The check came, and Arnold instinctively reached for it. He paid the bill, and the two men said their good-byes with a warm handshake.

It should have been nothing more than a memorable evening, a dream come true for Tiger. But two weeks later, he was called into the athletic office at school. He had violated NCAA rules again, accepting dinner from Arnold Palmer. The $25 dinner was classified as a gift, and college athletes weren't allowed to take any gifts. He was being suspended from playing golf until the NCAA could decide what to do about the violation. Tiger offered to send a check to Arnold. The NCAA agreed that Tiger's suspension would be lifted once the check cleared.

Two days later, Tiger traveled to El Paso for the Savane College All-America Golf Tournament, although he didn't know if he'd be able to play. Arnold Palmer had to cash the check, and then the bank would have to send a fax of the canceled check to NCAA headquarters. Tiger didn't think all this could possibly happen before the tournament, so he planned to fly back to Stanford without playing. Minutes before the tournament started, Tiger got the good news: The check had cleared. He ended up winning the tournament in a playoff.

In the press conference after the tournament, a visibly agitated Tiger was candid about his annoyance. "I was pretty angry," he said. "I felt like I didn't do anything wrong. By having dinner and talking about things I wanted to talk to him about, I'm told I'm going to be declared ineligible." When a reporter asked if the additional NCAA scrutiny might make him drop out of college to go pro, Tiger was ambivalent for the first time. "I don't think it would," he said, "but you never know. It's annoying."

Tiger was especially annoyed when Stanford officials questioned him about the source of a new set of irons he was using; the implication was that someone had given him the clubs as an undeclared gift. They also questioned him about his new brand of golf balls; they weren't the standard university issued brand. Was someone sponsoring him?

Tiger felt that the scrutiny was insulting and unfair; he was being singled out because of his high profile. He knew—as did everyone else—that he could renounce his amateur status at any time, go pro, and become very wealthy. Earl spoke to the media and estimated that Tiger could get up to $25 million in endorsements if he chose to go pro. It was a laughable number—no one would give Tiger Woods that much money—but the point was well taken. He would play through his sophomore year, he thought, and then he'd see what happened.

One thing was perfectly clear: Stanford needed Tiger Woods much more than Tiger Woods needed Stanford.

By the time he was fourteen, Tiger was
spending several hours per week on the
golf course, but he always maintained that
he was not pressured by Earl. "Don't force
your kids into sports," Tiger told *Golf*
magazine in 2000. "I never was. To this
day, my dad has never asked me to go play
golf. I ask him." (*Getty Images*)

At age fifteen years, six months, and twenty-eight days, Tiger became the youngest winner of the USGA Junior Amateur Championship. He would win the tournament for three consecutive years, becoming the only player to have won the championship more than once. (*Getty Images*)

By 1995, Tiger had amassed an impressive collection of trophies, and he kept them at his childhood home in Cypress, California. The trophies stayed in the home with Earl Woods even after Kultida moved to a larger house several miles away. (*Sports Illustrated/ Getty Images*)

"We did it, Pop," Tiger whispered to Earl during their emotional embrace at the 1997 Masters. Not only was Tiger the first African American or Asian winner of the tournament, but at age twenty-one he was also the youngest winner in Masters history.
(*Sports Illustrated/Getty Images*)

By early 2010, Tiger had seventy-one PGA Tour wins, including fourteen majors, but he always referred to his groundbreaking 1997 Masters win as the greatest victory in his career. As Nick Faldo put the green jacket on Tiger for the first time, "everything was just a blur," Tiger later said. "It was just a perfect moment." (*Associated Press*)

In January 1998, Earl and Kultida Woods were both in Phuket, Thailand, to watch Tiger win the Johnnie Walker Classic at Blue Canyon Golf Club. Over the years, Tiger would return to Thailand several times, saying that he felt a deep connection to his mother's native country. (*Getty Images*)

"My dad was my best friend and greatest role model," Tiger said after Earl's death in May 2006. "He was an amazing dad, coach, mentor, soldier, husband and friend." After the burial services, Tiger, Elin, and Kultida Woods attended a wake at the Tiger Woods Learning Center in Anaheim. (*Associated Press*)

The first few years of Tiger and Elin's marriage were glamorous and exciting, full of celebrity friends, fancy dinners, and public appearances such as the February 2006 dedication ceremony at the Tiger Woods Learning Center. Despite their lavish lifestyle, both Tiger and Elin insisted that they were the happiest during movie and video game marathons in their living room.
(*Wireimage*)

To create the imagery of Tiger walking on water for a commercial, EA Sports constructed a Plexiglas bridge in the middle of an Orlando lake. The videogame maker, which paid Tiger $20 million per year, would be one of the few sponsors to stand by Tiger after the scandal. (*Photo courtesy of Preston Mack*)

Tiger became close friends with several athletes, including Michael Jordan, who watched Tiger play during the practice round of the President's Cup golf tournament in October 2009. Jordan attended Tiger's wedding to Elin and later became a source of encouragement for Tiger after the scandal broke. (*Photo courtesy of Kyle Terada*)

Just six days before the accident that would set the scandal in motion, Tiger, Elin, and Sam attended an NCAA college football game at Stanford. Although they stayed for most of the game, Tiger and Elin interacted very little. (*Associated Press*)

Tiger and Elin's eight-bedroom, nine-bathroom lakefront home was the scene of the bizarre car accident on November 27, 2009. The next day Elin's Buick sat in front of the house while Tiger went into hiding. (*Photo courtesy of the Florida Highway Patrol/Corporal Tom Dewitt*)

Tiger's 2009 Escalade sustained more than $8,000 in damages during the accident, including two smashed rear windows. The police later suggested that Elin had smashed the windows with a golf club to free Tiger from the wreckage. Tiger claimed that she "acted courageously" and that any allegations of a domestic violence incident were "false, unfounded and malicious." (*Photo courtesy of the Florida Highway Patrol/Corporal Tom Dewitt*)

Rachel Uchitel was the first woman publicly linked to Tiger, and she became a central figure in the sex scandal. In November 2009, the *National Enquirer* alleged that Uchitel, a New York nightclub hostess, had hooked up with Tiger when he was in Melbourne to compete in the Australian Masters. Uchitel neither confirmed nor denied the rumors. (*Associated Press*)

"I'm so proud of you," Kultida Woods whispered to Tiger as he hugged her immediately after his February 2010 public statement. "Never think you stand alone. Mom will always be there for you and I love you." (*Associated Press*)

As of 2010, Tiger held the number one position in the world rankings for the most consecutive weeks and the greatest total number of weeks. He has been the year-end number one ranked golfer eleven times. (*Photo courtesy of Scott A. Miller*)

CHAPTER 7

THERE'S OFTEN AN EXPECTANT PAUSE as someone approaches a microphone, and the crowd of about one hundred touring pros, fans, and media lowered their voices to a dull murmur as Tiger Woods cleared his throat to speak at the Brown Deer Park Golf Club in Milwaukee. It was August 28, 1996, Tiger's first time speaking as a professional golfer—a historic moment, really, for those inclined to ascribe a greater meaning to the event. The assembled crowd waited in anticipation, wondering if he would have something profound to say. As Tiger silently stood in front of the audience, for a split second he looked less like a professional golfer and more like an average kid on any college campus around the country. He was wearing a black-and-yellow polo shirt—he hadn't yet committed himself to wearing his trademark red—and his hair was matted down from the Nike hat he had just removed. His baby face made him look younger than his twenty years, and he sat in front of a backdrop with a Miller Lite logo—a beverage he wouldn't be able to legally drink for several months.

"Hello, World," Tiger said, flashing the toothy smile that would soon become universally famous. The statement—simple in its structure but brash in its attitude—elicited a low chuckle from those assembled. Under the circumstances, this was an appropriate phrase, but it was hardly an ad-lib. Earlier that day, Nike had unveiled an ad campaign starring Tiger that used those exact same words. A three-page ad ran in the *Wall Street Journal,* and an accompanying television commercial would soon become ubiquitous on ESPN.

It was a synergistic day for Tiger and Nike; on the morning of Tiger's press conference, Nike released a statement confirming that Tiger would be its newest pitchman, and the company made no bones about its expectations for the young rookie. "Tiger Woods will have a tremendous impact on the world of sports and will change the way people view the game of golf," Nike chairman and CEO Phillip Knight said in a press release. "He is one of a handful of special athletes who transcend their sports, the way Jordan has done in basketball, and McEnroe did in tennis."

Whether or not the world was ready for Tiger, the golfing community had been waiting for a savior, someone who would coalesce a mainstream fan base. Tiger looked like the messiah golfers had been waiting for, and he quickly became the talk of the 1996 Greater Milwaukee Open, drawing an expectant crowd eager to see if he was really as good as he was rumored to be. He was touted—by sponsors, by golfers, even by the PGA itself—as the heir apparent, the man-child who would soon become golf's most famous icon.

It seemed unlikely that Tiger would fulfill all the expectations. He looked so young as he stood in front of the crowd, certainly not like the future of golf. During his six-minute press conference, Tiger told the crowd that his goal for the week was to win the tournament. After all, he reasoned aloud, why would anyone enter a competition if he didn't plan to win? It was a legitimate question, one that no one could really answer, but it also ruffled the feathers of some of the golfing elite. Tiger was straddling the thin line between confidence and cockiness, which would earn him both ardent fans and rabid detractors. His self-assurance was unmistakable; he spoke as if he had been making public appearances all his life, each word rolling off his tongue crisply and deliberately, with no sign of uncertainty.

He may have been brand new to the pro circuit, but the majority of the audience had more than a vague awareness of the Tiger Woods mystique. It had started as a low drone before escalating into a loud buzz: He was a gifted player with the potential to become one of the best athletes the sport had ever known. With a mixture of awe and jealousy, the golfing community whispered about Tiger's eye-catching endorsement deals: $20 million with the golf equipment giant Titleist and, of course, a five-year, $40 million deal with Nike. The deals had been signed before Tiger had hit a single ball professionally, and time would tell whether these companies were being reckless or prescient.

He wasn't a star yet, at least not officially, but an eleven-member entourage surrounded Tiger as he arrived in Milwaukee. His parents were there, of course, but so were reps for all the companies that owned a piece of him: three agents from IMG, a Titleist rep, and a Nike rep. The rest of his entourage comprised personal employees: his sports psychologist, his attorney, his coach, and an LA-based publicist. The members of his entourage were cogs in the machinery of the fledgling Tiger Woods brand, each with specific responsibilities and functions.

Few things would cause Tiger more consternation over the years than his relationship with the media, and his auspicious beginning was the first event in a long line of media frenzies. Throngs of reporters wrote about his background, some accurately and some erroneously, with the level of breathlessness that accompanies the emergence of a superstar.

Even the usually staid golf writers served up superlatives, declaring Tiger Woods the new face of golf as they posited unanswerable rhetorical questions about his impact. How would his middle-aged white competitors respond to him? Would Tiger's endorsement millions dull his competitive edge, making him unconcerned about missed putts? He had yet to hit a single ball, yet analysts heralded him as the future of the sport. How could anyone live up to those expectations?

There was no denying the sociological impact

of Tiger Woods, at least in the predominantly white sport of golf. Just six years earlier, the PGA had still been sanctioning events at courses that excluded blacks, and now the most exciting player in decades was a young African American. It was a seismic cultural shift, a visible indication that the sport had already changed, regardless of how well Tiger performed.

Although he hadn't yet played a single round, Tiger's skills weren't in question. His impressive amateur record laid the foundation for the escalating buzz, and all indications were that he was a special golfer, one with an uncanny ability to control the ball with a precision that escaped even the most seasoned golfers. Some of his abilities were natural and instinctive, of course, but relentless practice had honed his skills into remarkable exactitude. Focused correctly, Tiger could be a force in golf for decades.

As the crowd of reporters sat on white folding chairs in front of Tiger, they listened intently to each meticulously chosen word. The only sound in the room, other than Tiger's deliberate voice, was the click of flashbulbs. The moment was too significant for the sports pages; it was bigger than golf. Tiger Woods's decision to go pro would find its way into the front section of newspapers around the country. As Tiger finished speaking, the spectators exhaled almost collectively, as if they were suddenly cognizant that they had been listening to someone who would redefine how they thought of the game.

Decked out in Nike apparel from head to toe, Earl Woods was silently sitting beside his son. After Tiger was done speaking, Earl leaned into the microphone. "There is no comprehension by anyone on the impact this kid is going to have, not only on the game of golf, but on the world itself," he said grandiosely. "The Lord sent him here on a mission and it will transcend the game." Earl went on to claim that Tiger would eventually be bigger than Arthur Ashe and Muhammad Ali. He then told reporters that, given a choice, he would not have fathered another child at age forty-three. But Kultida's Thai culture necessitated a pregnancy, he explained, and "I don't shoot blanks."

It was classic Earl Woods: oversharing braggadocio that reflected his deep pride in his son. The brash statements hovered uneasily in the air for a few moments, then landed with a thud. Everything about the moment was wrong: the bragging, the proclamations of preordination, even the Nike hat. Onlookers looked away, embarrassed for Earl Woods and, more tangibly, embarrassed for Tiger. Earl evoked painful memories of tennis dad Stefano Capriati, who had turned his daughter Jennifer into a phenomenon when she was fourteen and burned her out three years later. Although both Tiger and Earl would consistently deny that Earl was a Svengali, it was a stereotype that would follow him for the rest of his life. Earl would become part of Tiger lore, not only because of his influence on his son, but also because these press conferences made him an indelible presence on the PGA Tour.

It was no accident that Tiger chose the Greater Milwaukee Open for his professional debut. It was a minor tournament, and only four of the sport's top thirty moneymakers could find time in their schedules to trek to Wisconsin to compete. Golf's biggest names would be absent, making Tiger the tournament's marquee star by default. With only seventy-six golfers making the cut, Tiger stood a good chance of placing high on the leaderboard; a strong showing would make a statement that he was golf's newest force.

But the most carefully constructed plans can be unraveled by bad bounces, missed putts, and blown concentration. It wasn't just that Tiger played poorly; he played frenetically, often seeming frazzled and preoccupied as he stumbled through the course. His long game was acceptable, but his medium-range putts consistently slipped past the cup as he struggled to pull out from the lower echelon of the leaderboard.

Despite his poor showing, Tiger still attracted a large and diverse crowd that waited expectantly for some sort of fireworks, some indication that Tiger Woods would be golf's first crossover superstar. And it happened, during the last round of the tournament. Somewhat improbably, on the 188-yard fourteenth hole, Tiger narrowed his stance and drew back his six iron, launching a knockdown shot that landed on the right side of the green, took one hop to the left, and rolled into the hole like a chip shot. The crowd erupted into raucous cheers, and for the first time in several rounds, Tiger smiled and waved at the assembled crowd. His messiah moment had happened, and the crowd had become his converts. It was a moment that defined the paradox of Tiger Woods: Even in defeat, he was a winner.

But a hole in one couldn't compensate for his faltering play, and Tiger finished in a tie for sixtieth place, pocketing $2,544 and finishing twelve strokes behind winner Loren Roberts. It was a stunning disappointment for Tiger, who had mentally prepared himself to win.

To many onlookers, it appeared that the overwhelming hype had eclipsed Tiger's abilities. Sure, he was a gifted golfer, but did he have the focus and mental acuity to win tournaments? It wouldn't be the first time that corporate America had thrown a bunch of money at an athlete, only to have him choke. Pundits wondered aloud if Tiger Woods could live up to the promise or if he would squander his potential before his career even began.

It was a discouraging loss for Tiger, who watched his bravado evaporate with each round. He hugged Earl Woods, softly apologizing for the loss. "I'm sorry, Pop," he whispered, the corners of his mouth drooping as he tried not to cry.

Earl put his hands on both sides of Tiger's head. Holding Tiger's face a foot away from his own, he looked deeply and meaningfully into his eyes. "I'm proud of you," he said simply, as he brought Tiger into his chest for a bear hug. It was a moment that went far deeper than wins and losses; Earl would be proud of Tiger whether or not he ever won a tournament. Of course, he would prefer for Tiger to win, but putting pressure on his son would be counterproductive, adding a nervous dimension to future tourneys. Earl had decided to be a rock of support no matter how Tiger played. He knew that the experience had taken the wind out of Tiger's sails, sending tremors of doubt through his son's mind. But it was one tournament and a minor one at that. Tiger would recover. He had the ability to be great; all he needed was the confidence. And besides, it might have been a good thing for Tiger to lose; he was so competitive that the embarrassment might inspire him to raise his game.

The loss did little to derail Tiger's endorsement deals. He had something that ran much deeper than his golfing skills, at least in the minds of corporate executives: Tiger Woods was immensely marketable. It wasn't just that he was a handsome and charismatic young man. Those traits boosted his marketability, of course, but there were hundreds of other attractive young athletes out there.

Tiger was breaking racial barriers, which gave him the aura of a trailblazer, an intangible commodity that made him even more attractive to corporations. Over the next few years, General Motors, General Mills, American Express, and Accenture lined up to pay millions to the young golfer.

On September 5, Tiger flew to Ancaster, Ontario, to compete in the Bell Canadian Open. Rain drizzled miserably on the greens of Hamilton Golf and Country Club, and each of Tiger's steps left a watery footprint in the grass. It was like walking on a soggy sponge, and officials shortened the tournament to fifty-four holes. Tiger finished at an eight-under-par 208, just six strokes behind winner Dudley Hart. More importantly, at least in Tiger's mind, was that he finished two strokes ahead of Loren Roberts, who had soundly beaten him at the Milwaukee Open. Tiger finished in eleventh place, a reassuring showing that proved to him, and everybody else, that he belonged in this world and was able to compete against other top golfers. The $37,500 he collected was secondary, a nearly insignificant perk of finishing.

A week later, Tiger flew to Illinois for the Quad City Classic, where he came close to victory for the first time in his professional career. The tournament seemed to be going his way; as he headed into the final round, he had a one-stroke lead over eventual winner Ed Fiori. Tiger was poised to win his first tournament, but a disastrous quadruple bogey on the fourth hole shook his focus, and he tied for fifth place.

At the following week's B.C. Open, another rainy week shortened the tournament, and Tiger finished the fifty-four holes at a thirteen-under-par 200, just three strokes behind winner Fred Funk. It was good enough to tie for third.

In just four PGA Tour events, Tiger had evolved from a struggling T-60 to an emerging contender, rising from eleventh to fifth to third. Tiger Woods was a juggernaut, a rapidly approaching freight train with an ultimate destination of victory. Winning seemed imminent, and it seemed to be much closer than anyone—except for Tiger and Earl Woods—could have possibly expected.

Not everyone was happy with the transformation that Tiger brought with him to the PGA, even though many of the changes were not his fault. Some of the other players resented the crowds that Tiger drew: people who didn't know much about golf, who didn't understand its polite decorum. Tiger had fans—loud ones who cheered his every move—and they proved distracting and intrusive to some of the more well-heeled players. No one on the tour complained that many of the new fans were black, at least not publicly. But before Tiger Woods, the gallery had been a sea of middle-aged white faces; now, there were minorities mixed in.

Tiger's year got even better in October, as he played the Las Vegas Invitational. He was four stokes behind the leader as he entered the last round; he seemed destined to finish somewhere in the top five. But something clicked, and Tiger played an inspired round, shooting a 64—the lowest score of any of the seventy-nine competitors. His amazing round forced a playoff with Davis Love, who failed to get up and down from a greenside bunker on the first extra hole. Tiger had played a grand total of five professional tournaments and had won his first one before his twenty-first birthday. "It's been an unbelievable experience," a beaming Tiger told reporters after the tournament. "It's just like winning the Amateur, though."

A second tournament in October etched Tiger Woods into the national consciousness when he won the Walt Disney World/Oldsmobile Classic in Orlando, beating Payne Stewart by a stroke. *Sports Illustrated* named Tiger its 1996 Sportsman of the Year and the PGA named him Rookie of the Year. Not yet twenty-one, Tiger had burst onto the scene like no other golfer, or any other athlete, had done before.

Even in the mid-1990s, some Americans were unwilling to watch a man of color on the golf course, and Tiger started receiving an alarming amount of hate mail from bigots enraged to see him encroaching on what had previously been a white man's sport. Some letters came to him care of the PGA Tour, whereas others came to his office and even to his home. Using venomous racial terms, some letters were ugly yet harmless, calling him a "nigger" and telling him to go back to Africa. Other letters were more worrisome, threatening Tiger with bodily harm. The letters affected Tiger profoundly; he had experienced racism throughout his life, but he had always believed that the bigots could be encouraged to accept him if he just worked hard enough. For the first time, he realized that no matter what he did or how hard he worked, there would be people who hated him simply because he was not white. He stopped reading his own mail before his team screened it. Tiger got the fan letters. The harmless hate mail went into a file for future reference. The threatening letters went to the FBI.

Perhaps no one was more alarmed at the hate mail than Tiger's parents. Kultida, while worried about Tiger's safety, was largely inclined to ignore the threats. They were just words, and obsessing about them would not benefit anyone. It was Kultida, not Earl, who encouraged Tiger to let the criticism roll off his back, considering the source. They were bigots who had nothing better to do than insult him for his skin color. She encouraged Tiger to be strong and focus on his game, not on the people who hated him. But Earl Woods knew the threat of racism; he had seen it before, and he knew that it never ended well. He worried about security around Tiger and how to neutralize the threats against him. Security at PGA events was relaxed; there had never been a reason to be worried about violent incidents during the tournaments, and most of the players never gave safety a second thought. But Earl knew that the threat was very real, and he convinced Tiger's team to develop a security plan for the golfer. Quietly and discretely, the team hired armed guards to watch Tiger as he walked the fairways. No one made a big deal about the bodyguards; letting the public know that his managers were worried would just exacerbate the problem and might paint Tiger as an overwrought diva. The security team kept such a low profile that even Tiger forgot that it was there.

With his newfound fame, Tiger quickly figured out a way to insulate himself from the media. He talked with his father and decided that certain parts of his life were not for public consumption. Of course, the media and fans could keep track of his golf career; that was to be expected. But Tiger's home life—the thing he found most sacred—would be kept private.

Whenever a new superstar emerges, public curiosity surrounds him (or her) and reporters want to learn about every aspect of the star's life. With Tiger Woods, the curiosity became deafening; he was an enigma to everyone, even other golfers. His race, his background, his relationship with his father . . . it was all a curiosity, and the media scrambled to learn more about him.

Tiger assembled a team to help him create a public persona that would be simultaneously engaging and aloof, relatable and superior. He hired Hughes Norton, a graduate of Harvard Business School, as his agent. One of IMG's top agents, Hughes had been in sports marketing for nearly twenty-five years; he knew his way around a negotiation table. Hughes had aggressively negotiated the Nike deal; he was known for demanding, and getting, whatever his clients wanted. Hughes was not a warm and fuzzy guy; he could be prickly and aggressive, but he was exactly what Tiger needed. Tiger knew that Hughes had his back, making sure that no one would tarnish his image and jeopardize his status as a cash cow, both for the PGA Tour and for his endorsement deals.

Tiger also hired Bev Norwood as his spokesman and media liaison. Bev had been in the business for nearly two decades; he would be Tiger's gatekeeper, holding the media in line and guarding Tiger's reputation. Tiger's image was safe.

"WHAT I CAN'T FIGURE OUT," Tiger said with a smirk, "is why so many good-looking women hang around baseball and basketball. Is it because, you know, people always say that, like, black guys have big dicks?"

It was guy talk, a question that wouldn't have raised eyebrows in a frat house or locker room. But this was Tiger Woods, golf's newest phenomenon, and he wasn't in a frat house or locker room; he was in the back of a limo, bantering with the burly driver on his way to a photo shoot for *GQ* magazine. And next to him, furiously taking notes, was writer Charles P. Pierce.

During his day with Pierce, Tiger told jokes about Jesus and golf, black guys and condoms. He was relaxed, having a good time, saying things that he shouldn't say in front of a reporter. He looked over and saw Pierce taking copious notes.

"Hey, you can't write this," he protested.

"Too late," Pierce replied.

The story hit the stands in April 1997, and it immediately caused a sensation. Tiger Woods, the squeaky-clean wunderkind of golf, had more than a dirty mouth; he had a dirty mind, and he seemed preoccupied with the penis size of black men.

It was a flash of controversy that was gone almost before it started, leaving no scars or permanent damage. Tiger would escape this minor storm unscathed; the American public was fine with a few dirty jokes, and they only reinforced the public perception of Tiger: so young, so naïve, and so normal.

But within Tiger's camp, the incident became a turning point for Tiger's managers, a distinct change in how they dealt with the press. Tiger needed protection from himself; he was too green to fully comprehend the concept of "off the record." As a direct result of the controversial interview, Tiger's publicity team started to play hardball with journalists, golf writers, and celebrity reporters alike. If a reporter wrote something that displeased Tiger, or anyone at IMG, he or she would be excommunicated from Tiger's inner circle, and Tiger would never speak to that reporter again. It was a threat that scared most reporters into sticking with the party line, censoring themselves on everything they wrote. Losing access to Tiger, especially for sportswriters, could be a disastrous blow to a career.

Tiger's team would never approach a writer and tell him or her what to write; that would be too meddlesome, too obvious. But his managers gave guidelines to reporters, micromanaging the stories until they read like Tiger Woods advertorials: glowing, positive puff pieces that promoted whatever it was that Tiger wanted to promote. If writers ran too far afoul, they would be unceremoniously dumped; Tiger's team would not return calls, interview requests would be rejected, and access would be blocked. Journalists who wrote positive pieces that weren't exactly to Tiger's specifications would get calm, deliberate phone calls from members of the team, reminding them that Tiger had a long memory and that he was "very disappointed" in the story. There would be no yelling, no insults. The excommunication was as cool and methodical as an exceptionally effective mob hit.

Writers would good-naturedly compare notes about their run-ins with Tiger's team, but no one ever suspected that Tiger or his managers were trying to hide any skeletons in his closet. They just seemed to be meticulously crafting the image of a man who was on the fast track to greatness. "There was a sense of, 'Well, they're protecting their brand,'" says golf writer Tom Cunneff. "There wasn't a sense of, 'What are they trying to hide?' Everyone wanted a piece of Tiger, and it just made sense that they were trying to protect him."

In a remarkably short stretch of seven tournaments, Tiger earned enough money to finish in the top thirty on the money list. He easily qualified for the Tour Championship. If there was a downside to his amazing year, it occurred shortly after 2:00 a.m. on a Friday in October 1996. The second round of the Tour Championship was going to start the next morning, and Earl Woods was rushed to a Tulsa hospital complaining of chest pains and shortness of breath, later revealed as a heart attack. Earl demanded that Kultida not call Tiger; he didn't want to worry his son. But Kultida had other ideas, and she called Tiger in the middle of the night, causing the young golfer to rush to his father's side. Tiger was more terrified than Earl. To come this far and lose his father was unthinkable, and Tiger considered withdrawing from the tournament. But Earl had other plans and sent Tiger back to the links, where he finished tied for twenty-first place.

Earl, now sixty-four, had a triple bypass, which would weaken him considerably, slowing him down for the rest of his life. But he was going to be okay, and by the time Tiger left Southern Hills, he knew that a disaster had been averted and that he hadn't lost Earl.

Tiger desperately and profoundly wanted Earl to be present as he played the Masters in April 1997. Even playing in the tournament—his first major as a pro—would be a dream come true. The Masters clubhouse was a symbol of privilege that had a long tradition of exclusion. For decades, black players had been prohibited from playing the greens of Augusta; the closest that an African American could come to the course was to work in the clubhouse kitchen. In 1975, Lee Elder became the first black player to play at the Masters, breaking through the barrier of bigotry. It was a proud moment for Elder, but change followed slowly, more like a steady drip than a rushing river. Augusta National admitted its first black member fifteen years later, in 1990. By 1997, only four black players had ever been invited to play the Masters. Tiger would become the fifth.

He arrived in Augusta with his caddy, Mike "Fluff" Cowan. At forty-nine years old, Fluff had the knowledge and experience that Tiger lacked; he and Tiger had become friends and confidants. They thought as a team, with the precision of a doctor and nurse operating on a patient; Tiger gave Fluff the respect he deserved, and Fluff gave Tiger the tools he needed. Fluff knew the courses;

he would be a steadying influence on Tiger for the biggest tournament of his young career.

Tiger's competing at Augusta hit all the right notes in the media: The phenomenon would now compete in golf's most revered tournaments. It didn't matter that Tiger was only twenty-one. It didn't matter that he had been on the tour for less than a year. Tiger Woods was expected to do well, to win if possible. The media applied pressure on him, noting that blacks would be watching, that the world would be watching, and that Tiger had better not let them down.

There was never much doubt that Tiger was going to win the Masters, at least once he started playing. Blocking out the screaming crowds, the demanding media, and his own self-doubt, Tiger never let anyone come closer than the nine-shot lead that he carried into the final round. If he had been a different player, a middle-aged white man, the tournament would have been boring; the ending a foregone conclusion, and there would have been scant excitement. But the mere presence of Tiger Woods electrified the tourney; instead of the drama of competition, audiences focused on the historic journey unfolding before their eyes. Tiger Woods was about to break the color barrier in just his fifteenth tournament as a professional golfer.

As his flawless game progressed, Tiger dominated the course. The crowds watched under

Augusta's sunny skies as everything seemed to go Tiger's way, with each drive and each putt contributing to the growing narrative of Tiger's legend, accompanied by a soundtrack of boisterous cheering and standing ovations.

There were accolades and platitudes, tributes and awards. Serious reporters discussed the sociological ramifications of the win. Jubilant onlookers, including Lee Elder, cheered as Tiger approached the eighteenth hole, blinking back tears. As he sank the last putt, the score became official: Tiger had won the Masters with an exceptional score of 270, eighteen under par and twelve strokes ahead of runner-up Tom Kite.

Earl Woods wasn't supposed to be there. His triple bypass surgery had made him tired and lethargic, and doctors warned him that travel could cause undue strain on his heart. But Earl had the stubbornness that came with six decades of forging his own path; against doctor's orders, he had made the trek to Augusta to watch his son compete. It was a decision he would never regret, even if it killed him; it was non-negotiable.

After the win, Tiger embraced Fluff Cowan, maintaining his stoic composure until he saw his father. Breaking away from Fluff, he hugged Earl Woods tightly, realizing that he had fulfilled not only his own dreams but also his father's.

"I'm proud of you," Earl whispered, stroking his son's head. "Let it go. Let it go."

"We did it, Pop," Tiger answered softly, as the two men dissolved into tears. The cameras picked up the heartfelt moment, and for the first time the world got a glimpse of the close relationship between Tiger and Earl Woods. Although no one but the two men would ever understand the depth and complexity of their relationship, everyone could see that they were close, best friends who deeply loved each other.

As he gave his post-Masters interview to the assembled press, a composed and deliberate Tiger managed to control his exuberance as he explained how he had won. "My focus never left me," he said simply. "Even with all the emotion and everybody cheering me on, I knew I had to take care of business first." He was the youngest Masters winner in history, with decades ahead of him.

But the tournament was not without its controversy. After finishing in thirty-fourth place, Fuzzy Zoeller, with a drink in hand, approached reporters and jokingly made a comment about Tiger. Referring to the following year's Masters Champions Dinner—the menu would be chosen by the current year's winner—Zoeller said: "That little boy is driving well and he's putting well. He's doing everything it takes to win. So, you know what you guys do when he gets in there? You pat him on the back and say congratulations and enjoy it, and tell him not to serve fried chicken next year." He smiled, snapped his fingers, and walked away, then turned and added, "or collard greens or whatever the hell they serve."

The ensuing media frenzy was deafening, and Tiger was privately annoyed at the situation. He didn't care about what Zoeller had said; he recognized the spirit of the statements and wasn't offended. But the resulting media storm was a distraction, yet one more reminder that, even though Tiger was respected in the game, he wasn't considered just one of the guys. He was different, and people would continue to remind him of his difference.

Zoeller immediately apologized publicly for his statements, and then he started losing endorsement deals. K-mart and Dunlop both dropped him as a spokesman; racism was a touchy subject, and both sponsors wanted no part in the ensuing drama. Zoeller publicly claimed that the comments were misconstrued, that a racist meaning was inserted where there had been no obvious intent.

For his part, Tiger didn't make a public statement, allowing Zoeller to twist in the wind as his apology hung in the air, unaccepted. A month after the incident, Tiger finally sat down with Zoeller for a twenty-minute lunch, where he officially and publicly accepted the apology. The incident was behind them, but Tiger felt that it marred the Masters, inserting ugliness and misunderstanding into the biggest achievement of his life and career. This would be the first incident in what would become a pattern for Tiger, an expectation that he would sound off on matters of race and the PGA. It wasn't a role in which he felt comfortable; he just wanted to play golf, not be the poster boy for race relations. Although he would grow resigned to the role, he never quite understood or embraced it.

It was intended to be a comfortable interview, just a way for the American public to learn more about Tiger. Oprah Winfrey was the queen of talk, and she devoted an entire hour to Tiger Woods. Tiger and Earl flew to Chicago to make the appearance; it would be a positive experience without a hint of controversy.

"Growing up, I came up with this name. I'm a 'Cablinasian,'" Tiger said with a smile. The media picked up on his bizarre portmanteau, and Tiger's attempt to become postracial set off yet another discussion about racial identity.

The problem was that Tiger never really knew how much to divulge about his personal life; what he said could be misconstrued and twisted, and Tiger would end up being criticized for something he hadn't meant to say. Despite his extensive training in media relations, Tiger had a tendency to get carried away and say what he didn't really mean. His suspicion of the media extended to the production people on his commercials and video games; he just didn't know if they'd misrepresent him to the press.

"During down time on the shoots, we'd be

playing video games," says one television production source, "and Tiger would be having a great time. He'd start telling a lot of dirty jokes or making comments about the tight ass on some woman and then all of a sudden realize that he had gone too far. He would drop the video game controller on the floor and say, 'Um, I gotta go.' No good-byes, no anything. He'd just say something wrong and get the hell out of there."

Tiger had a sweaty sense of humor that made him popular with the guys; he could tell a dirty joke with a flourish, and he seemed to love shocking people with his raunch. "Yeah, he could swear a blue streak," says the production source. "Not just being vulgar, but being obscene, in a really funny way. If you could get him to trust you, he'd talk about anything: racial, sexual, religious jokes. I think he liked being irreverent because his life was so structured. It was a way for him to rebel."

The first half of 1997 continued to be successful for Tiger. In addition to winning the Masters, he also won the Mercedes Championship, the GTE Byron Nelson Golf Classic, and the Motorola Western Open. Television executives started noticing a ratings trend: When Tiger competed, the ratings spiked. He was valuable to the game of golf, bringing it an everyman appeal that it had previously lacked.

By June 15, less than a year after he had turned pro, Tiger rose to number one in the Official

World Golf Rankings. It was the fastest-ever ascent to the top spot, and the legend of Tiger Woods became even stronger. He had lived up to the hype, justifying his endorsement contracts and becoming the sport's first genuine crossover superstar. Everyone knew who Tiger Woods was; there were sports cards, bobblehead dolls, and personalized golf equipment. He began writing a golf instruction column for *Golf Digest* in 1997.

In less than a year, Tiger Woods had become a one-named legend like Michael Jordan or Lance Armstrong; his last name had almost become a vestige of his life before fame. Everyone knew who Tiger was; he was instantly recognizable and nearly universally adored. But despite his ubiquity, he remained aloof, mysterious, and tantalizingly beyond reach. He would have been accused of being robotic if it weren't for his temper, the under-the-breath "fucks" and "shits" that escaped his mouth during missed putts. But if uncensored expletives were the worst sins that Tiger committed, the sponsors could live with that; it just showed that he was a fierce competitor who profoundly wanted to win.

There was another benefit to superstardom, a perk that Tiger enjoyed. Women of all types followed Tiger on the course, sometimes lewdly propositioning him. Tiger preferred pretty Nordic-looking women with blonde hair and shapely figures. There was no shortage of these women, both on and off the golf course, and Tiger was often seen at clubs in Orlando, dirty dancing and making out with these women. It wasn't scandalous; he was rich and single, and he lived a playboy lifestyle expected of an athlete his age.

The constant stream of women wasn't an issue for Earl Woods, who himself had always had a soft spot for the ladies. He was proud of his son's prowess, although the two men developed a "don't ask, don't tell" policy about the women whom Tiger bedded. Earl knew there were women—lots of them—but he had no desire to hear every detail of his son's love life. But as pretty women swarmed around Tiger on the golf course, begging for autographs, Earl couldn't help but smile. "That's my boy," he smirked to whomever was nearby, jerking his thumb upward to point in Tiger's direction.

In some ways, it would have been unreasonable for Earl to expect Tiger to resist temptation, to ignore the women pleading for his attention. After all, he was young, handsome, and rich. He had no trouble finding women who were all too happy to have sex within minutes of meeting him; it was a perk of being a new superstar.

With expectations high, there was nowhere for Tiger to go but down. His play faded in the second half of 1997, and by 1998 he was experiencing his first career slump, winning only the BellSouth Classic. Critics started wondering whether he was a flash in the pan, a gifted golfer with no staying power. Tiger bristled when people wondered whether he had already peaked, and his management team went into overdrive, castigating any writers who dared to question Tiger's staying power. In general, golf writers were happy to stick to the Tiger narrative, despite his increasing number of losses. Tiger had been good to the sport and, by extension, to the golf writers who were enjoying increased expense accounts and salaries. It was in everyone's best interest to paint Tiger as a charismatic superstar who could do no wrong, even if the statistics contradicted the narrative. Besides, Tiger was still in his early twenties and navigating the early days of his career.

His slump didn't affect his image, and corporations clamored to partner with him. Video game maker EA Sports signed Tiger Woods in 1998 to be the face of its *PGA Tour Golf* game. He would become a two-dimensional character in the game, and players would be able to become Tiger Woods, at least on-screen. The game was a runaway success, with sales increasing by 150 percent in the first year. Tiger Woods was a valuable commodity, and corporations offered him millions to lend his face to their products. He had succeeded beyond his wildest dreams. He just needed someone to share all this with.

SHE WAS A PRETTY BLONDE CO-ED, a member of Pi Beta Phi sorority, a former high school cheerleader. She was popular on the campus of Cal–Santa Barbara, turning heads as she walked across campus in jeans and short T-shirts that showed off her curvy figure. But her legally blonde stereotype belied her intelligence and ambition: Joanna Jagoda was a political science major with ambitions of attending law school. She was no dumb blonde; she was a serious student who consistently made the dean's list.

It was a weird first date, set up by one of Joanna's sorority sisters. Tiger and Joanna met at the sorority house and spent the next two hours sitting at a table and talking with several of Joanna's starstruck sorority sisters. Amid the giggling sorority girls and awkward pauses, Tiger and Joanna clicked, and they began a relationship that many thought would end in marriage.

Their dating life was simultaneously glamorous and pedestrian. One weekend would be spent eating at chain restaurants, walking around the neighborhood, and watching movies. The next weekend would entail a flight to tournaments around the globe. It was a comfortable relationship, one that wasn't for public consumption. Tiger and Joanna were tight-lipped about the trajectory of their relationship, and tabloids constantly predicted that they would marry.

In 1999, Tiger returned to dominance, beginning a three-year winning streak that would cement his spot as one of golf's best players. In February, he won the Buick Invitational by two strokes. As the year went on, he won the Memorial Tournament and the Motorola Western Open.

In August 1999, Tiger beat Sergio Garcia by one stroke to win the PGA Championship, his second major and proof that he was here to stay; his slump had lasted less than two years, and he had roared back, at age twenty-three, to assert his dominance on the links. He won four more tournaments in 1999, claiming the top spot on the money list. By the time the dust had settled, he had notched eight wins during the year, including one major. The next year was going to be even better.

IT WAS REALLY AN INNOCUOUS interview, certainly not anything that could have been remotely considered scandalous. Fluff Cowan gave an interview to *Golf* magazine in 1999 and mentioned as an aside that he earned $1,000 a week with Tiger, plus bonuses of up to 10 percent of Tiger's winnings. Fluff had earned more than $200,000 in the previous year, not including his commercial endorsements and golfing videos.

But the interview would become a turning point in the relationship between Tiger and Fluff, just another source of friction that would never be completely resolved. They really were an odd couple—Tiger was tall and muscular; Fluff was short and round—but they had been a good team, a winning team, for twenty-nine months.

The speculation began when Tiger asked his childhood friend Bryon Bell to caddy for him during the 1999 Buick Invitational. The decision reverberated around the fairways, leading to speculation that something might be wrong. Finally, in March, Tiger abruptly and decisively fired Fluff, giving the older man no official reason for the decision. He then released a statement: "Fluff and I have discussed this over the past few weeks, and we both feel it is in our best interest to part ways. I appreciate the support which Fluff has provided and recognize the contributions Fluff has made to my success as a professional. But it is time to move on and I feel confident we will remain friends."

Tiger chose Steve Williams, a New Zealand caddy who had carried Raymond Floyd's bag for more than a decade, to become Fluff's successor. Steve would be his caddy for the next decade, and it would become a relationship based on unparalleled trust.

The turn of the century brought few changes to Tiger; he continued his dominance of the PGA Tour and had his best year ever in 2000. He would win three consecutive majors and nine PGA Tour events and set or tie twenty-seven tour records. He beat Ernie Els with a fifteen-stroke victory at the U.S. Open in June. The next month, he won the 2000 Open Championship by eight strokes. Less than a month later, he won the PGA Championship in a head-to-head playoff against Bob May. At age twenty-four, Tiger became the youngest golfer to achieve the career grand slam, having won all four of golf's major championships: the U.S. Open, the British Open, the PGA Championship, and the Masters. He was named the 2000 *Sports Illustrated* Sportsman of the Year, becoming the first and only athlete to be honored twice. *Golf Digest* ranked him as the twelfth best golfer of all time just four years after he had turned professional.

Tiger was quickly becoming a victim of his own dominance. Expectations were unreasonably high for him; both reporters and fans assumed that he'd win every tournament. He wasn't allowed to lose, or golf columns across the country would wonder what was happening to Tiger. To always be at the top of his game, unbeatable and dominant, was a stress Tiger put on himself. Tiger's temper became almost legendary, with strings of expletives accompanying most missed putts or bad tee shots. During one round at the 2000 U.S. Open, he hooked his tee shot into the Pacific Ocean. Visibly enraged, Tiger loudly yelled, "God damn it, you fucking prick." The gallery gasped, as did the control room of NBC, which aired the comments live on a Saturday morning. Tiger later apologized, but the damage had been done. Pundits criticized Tiger profusely. Golf was a gentleman's game, and that language would be unacceptable for any other player. He wasn't perfect after all.

As 2001 began, Tiger's winning streak continued

unbroken. His two-stroke win at the Masters marked the only time within the era of the modern grand slam that any player had held all four major championship titles at the same time. The feat was called the Tiger Slam. It was not a true grand slam, however, because it was not achieved in the same calendar year.

The rest of 2001 might have been called a mini-slump if Tiger hadn't achieved so much in the first part of the year. It wasn't that he played badly; it was just the effect of him coming back down from the stratosphere. He was playing like any other player, competently but not flawlessly. During the last half of the season, Tiger had a string of professional disappointments. He was not a factor in the three remaining majors of the year. Still, he finished with five PGA Tour wins in the season, the most of any player.

In 2002, he continued his dominance by winning the Masters for the third time. He was only the third golfer to win back-to-back Masters tournaments, and the win rekindled buzz about the calendar grand slam that had eluded him in 2000. He won the U.S. Open by three strokes that June, but fell short at the British Open Championship, when he shot an 81 in a disastrous third round. He hobbled through to the end of the year by losing the PGA Championship by one stroke. Little did he know that he was entering a slump, one that would last for two years.

CHAPTER 8

IT WASN'T A THROBBING PAIN, exactly, more of a dull ache that persisted, nagging at Tiger as if his left knee were constantly caught in an ever-tightening vise. If he moved his leg in just the wrong way, the dull ache would transform into a shooting pain that electrified his entire leg, radiating upward and causing him to wince. On good days, he would go for long periods without any pain at all, but one wrong move could lead to hours of stiffness and discomfort. He tried everything: ice, heat, balms, and painkillers. Nothing seemed to work, at least not as well as he hoped, and the fear of pain was always in the back of his mind. The same knee had given him trouble before. In 1994, when he was just eighteen, he had had surgery to remove a benign tumor, an operation that had threatened to end his golf career before it even began.

Tiger didn't plan to modify his swing in 2002; he was simply trying to give himself a little relief from the chronic pain. Tiger feared that the power behind his swing was destroying his knee; if he didn't make adjustments, he might never be golf's most dominant player again. He had always rotated his trunk forcefully; his pelvis would shift and transfer his full weight onto his left knee, straining the ligaments as he moved. The increasing pain forced him to alter his swing, slightly changing the way he pivoted. By the end of the 2002 season, Tiger's swing had morphed into a curious amalgamation of his old swing and what would ultimately become his new swing.

It had been a season of pain management for Tiger. He moved slowly and gingerly, always protecting his knee, yet bracing for the next stabbing pain. Before tournaments, he took painkillers in the hope that they would help, but he ended up grimacing his way through the last few holes.

In December 2002, near the end of the season, the pain grew to be too much, and Tiger finally had the arthroscopic surgery that he probably should have had months earlier. It was a successful surgery: Doctors drained excess fluid and removed a benign cyst from the knee. With the proper rest, Tiger would be as good as new. They sent him back to his Isleworth home to recover.

Days after the surgery, Tiger hobbled onto the golf course and tried to hit a few balls. He didn't hit many, and he didn't hit them far, but he didn't want to let his swing get rusty. As with most recoveries, each day was better than the day before, and Tiger disciplined himself to practice as much as he could. On February 13, 2003, just sixty-three days after his surgery, Tiger stepped up to the first tee at the Buick Invitational, improbably and surprisingly walking away with a win. His knee continued to heal, and Tiger worked on his swing to make sure his knee wouldn't be injured again. His old swing just wasn't working; if he continued to move that way, he'd be having knee surgery again in just a few years. It was time to figure out something new, perhaps a swing that would actually make Tiger an even better golfer. There would be a transitional period, but Tiger was determined to reap the long-term benefits of a change in his swing.

Other changes were looming in Tiger's life. The relationship with Joanna Jagoda wasn't working out. They had been together for three years—three happy years full of good dates and relaxing get-aways—but the relationship was going nowhere, and they both knew it. Not much needed to be said; the relationship had simply run its course, and Tiger was ready to move on. Quietly and soberly, without any fanfare, he ended things with Joanna.

If it was a difficult breakup, Tiger and Joanna didn't share their anguish with friends. Joanna moved her things out of Tiger's Florida home and returned to Malibu to attend Pepperdine School of Law; she had put her career on hold to be with Tiger, and she took the breakup as a sign that it was time to resume her studies. Tiger continued to work through his slumping career, practicing on his home course every day, often taking day trips to South Florida to see his friend Jesper Parnevik, who had the hottest nanny of any of the players on the Tour: a blonde beauty named Elin Nordegren.

THEY WANTED HIM TO SAY ANYTHING, to address the controversy. Journalists from around the country deluged the office of Mark Steinberg with calls and e-mails, asking for a comment that Tiger was unwilling and unable to give. Tiger had become golf's breakthrough kid, the person who had toppled so many barriers. Surely, he would have a comment about the latest: Feminist author and activist Martha Burk wanted Augusta National to admit women, and she waged a loud and highly publicized media campaign to convince the club to open its membership to both genders. After reading that Augusta didn't allow women, Burk, who had not played golf in more than twenty years, vowed to shake things up.

That June, Burk, who ran the National Council of Women's Organizations, had written a letter to Hootie Johnson, the outspoken chairman of Augusta National, urging him to allow women members. He refused to budge, issuing a statement to the media. "We will not be bullied," he wrote. "There may well come a day when women will be invited to join our membership, but not at the point of a bayonet." Augusta National was a private club, he maintained, and despite Burk's protests of sexism and transgressed civil rights, the club had a right to choose its own membership.

Burk upped the ante, stating that the Masters should not hold a tournament in a male-only club;

it was sexist, she believed, to exclude one gender from Augusta National. She announced her plans to picket the next Masters.

The controversy had very little to do with Tiger and everything to do with the sexual politics of golf. As reporters pressed him for a comment, Tiger remained noncommittal, refusing to open up about his beliefs. It was a difficult situation for him to navigate, and he expressed his feelings to friends about the controversy: No one asked Ernie Els or Mark O'Meara what he thought; why should Tiger be the only golfer required to go out on a limb to say something?

If anything, the pressure was a natural by-product of his celebrity. Tiger's barrier-breaking made him the go-to spokesperson for all issues of equality. His reticence to talk infuriated the media. When it became clear that Tiger would not weigh in on the controversy, the *New York Post* ran a full-page headline above Tiger's face. It consisted of one simple, cutting word: "Hypocrite."

Tiger was destroyed in editorials, berated by columnists, and pummeled by headline writers for nearly two months, accused of being a coward. Finally, in August, he fired back with a statement. "Everyone has to understand that Augusta isn't quick to change things," he said. "No matter what I or the press say, they do things at their own pace, such as allowing the first black golfer to play or join the club, and won't buckle to outside pressure.

Would I like to see women members? Yes, that would be great, but I am only one voice. I'm not even a regular member."

The statement pleased no one. Martha Burk told reporters that she wished Tiger would come out stronger to support her side. Hootie Johnson was even more scathing during a press conference several months later. "I won't tell Tiger how to play golf if he doesn't tell us how to run our private club," he said testily.

It was a hard lesson for Tiger, one that he wished he had learned earlier. As the world's most famous golfer, there are some luxuries he didn't have. Keeping silent was one of them; speaking out was another. Tiger privately bemoaned his no-win situation; no matter what he did to address the Martha Burk controversy, somebody would be offended. Still, it was easier to take the heat for not having an opinion than it was to be criticized for having the wrong one. He vowed to stay away from future controversies; they just weren't worth it. Besides, his statements didn't seem to make much difference: The controversy eventually blew over without Augusta admitting Burk or any other female members.

TIGER WASN'T ONE FOR LONG GOOD-BYES, in either his personal or professional life. When he was done with someone, when he or she could no longer be of any use to him, he would unceremoniously cut that person loose, sentiment be damned. Tiger decided he was done with Butch Harmon in 2003, and the ax swung quickly and permanently. Butch hadn't done anything; Tiger just felt he had learned all he needed to learn from Butch and that it was time to find a new swing coach.

It was an abrupt end to a long relationship that had benefited both men. Tiger was seventeen years old when Butch had started coaching him. Now, more than a decade later, Tiger decided to move in a different direction, and Butch was the casualty.

Butch's credentials were impeccable, the result of a lifetime of golf. He started attending golf tournaments at age five, when his father, Claude, won the Masters. Butch grew up on golf courses, and after serving in the Vietnam War, he became a PGA Tour player. As a coach, he worked with Greg Norman, taking him to the number one position in the world.

Butch's credentials were impressive, but his results with Tiger had been even more awe inspiring. The two began working together in 1993, and their partnership helped Tiger win three straight U.S. Amateur titles and eight majors. The swing that Tiger and Butch developed was intimidating in its dominance, helping Tiger win his first Masters by an impressive twelve strokes. Butch had been by Tiger's side in 2000 when Tiger devastated the competition, winning the British Open by eight shots and the U.S. Open by an unfathomable fifteen strokes. Butch also came at a bargain price: Tiger paid him only $50,000 per year.

But Tiger was ready to move on. Before the PGA Championship in 2002, he kept Butch at arm's length, not allowing him to come on the course. It was obvious to everyone, including Butch, that he was going to be phased out. As the two kept in sporadic contact into the 2003 season, it was clear that they were at the end of their working relationship. After a few sessions in July 2003, Tiger cut ties with Butch and replaced him with Hank Haney.

Publicly, Tiger and Butch explained the split as cordial, even amicable. The official party line was that it was just time for both men to move on, to try new things. No hard feelings. That was the way it always was with Tiger: Splits were amicable; disagreements were minor; rifts were nonexistent. In Tiger Woods's world, no feelings were ever hurt; no one was ever angry or sad about the splits. They were just cordial business decisions.

Privately, however, Butch was hurt that Tiger would push him aside after everything they had weathered together. It wasn't just that he was fired; it was how he was fired, being phased out slowly, with the people around Tiger disingenuously telling Butch that nothing was wrong, that the awkwardness was all in his head. In reality, Butch was deeply hurt, and the disappointment morphed into anger. A few months later, Tiger told reporters that he had forgotten 90 percent of what Butch had taught him, retaining just the useful 10 percent. The insult stung Butch, who was still unaware of why he had been dismissed. He groused about it to anyone who would listen; he felt disrespected and unappreciated. Their friendship had cooled; whereas Tiger seemed to move past the split easily, Butch stayed wounded.

Tiger was still one of golf's top contenders, but something was missing in his game. His long game was still weak; his new swing was progressing nicely, but it still wasn't giving him the power or the accuracy to play up to his best capability. Although he won several smaller tournaments, Tiger was unable to win a major in 2003 or 2004. He had slumped before, but this one was unlike the previous valleys in his career, both in its severity and its duration. His previous declines had lasted for only a few months; this was a prolonged drought that surprised Tiger. He expected that his swing change would result in some difficult hurdles, but even he hadn't expected to fall back to earth so quickly.

The speculation began as it always did, with commentators dissecting Tiger's struggles. Was it his split with Butch Harmon? Another injury? His new swing? Tiger largely ignored the speculation, although one of the theories bothered him more than the others. His slump coincided with his relationship with Elin Nordegren, and people were saying that she was the Delilah to his

Sampson, the one who could sap his energy and competitive drive. It wasn't true, of course, but the rumors spread throughout the golf media. As always, Tiger refused to say anything publicly. Let people speculate, he thought. He needed to work on his game.

Every hero needs a villain, someone to challenge him and goad him on to greatness. For years, Tiger had been a man without a nemesis; his presence on the golf course was intimidating to his competitors, and few of them presented a consistent challenge to him. Tiger stood alone at the head of the pack; there had really been no one in his league.

Tiger had spent 264 consecutive weeks as the world's top-ranked golfer, a record that was stunning in its longevity. Upon landing the top spot in 1999, Tiger was untouchable; no one was any-where close to toppling him. But as the slump dragged on, Tiger's hold on the world's top ranking became tenuous. He needed to win something major to maintain his spot. The wins didn't come, and the Deutsch Bank Championship in September 2004 changed the landscape of the game. Tiger finished at T-2, three strokes behind Vijay Singh, a forty-one-year-old Fijian who had become a strikingly steady and reliable player. For the first time in more than five years, Tiger slipped to number two in the rankings, bested only by Singh.

On paper, Vijay could have been a dramatic rival for Tiger, a character that the PGA could have promoted to spark some interest in the first real challenge that Tiger had faced in years. Vijay was a brusque, abrasive player who spoke his mind, often bluntly. The year before claiming the top spot, he had courted his own controversy with a series of politically incorrect statements about women golfers. LPGA player Annika Sorenstam had received a sponsor's exemption to become the first woman in nearly fifty years to play a PGA Tour event. She would play in the Bank of America Colonial tournament, a controversial decision that was loudly heralded, yet whisperingly criticized in the golf community. Although many golfers chose not to address the controversy, Vijay brazenly spoke out. In an interview with the Associated Press, Vijay said that Annika didn't belong on the links with men. If he was paired with her, Vijay said in his typically caustic way, he would withdraw from the tournament.

It was a controversial interview, especially given the climate of golf after the Martha Burk controversy. The idea of women playing in men's golf tournaments was in the national consciousness, and Vijay's comments further stoked the debate. Golf had changed, commentators maintained. It was now a sport that included people who had historically been denied a spot on the PGA tour:

people like Annika, Tiger, and dark-skinned Vijay.

Controversy is good, at least when it comes to television ratings, but Vijay simply wasn't charismatic enough to be the PGA villain to Tiger Woods's Superman. He was reticent to talk about himself to the press, and, justifiably or not, he had been labeled dull. He was consistent and efficient on the course, but neither his skills nor his persona translated into a compelling narrative that could spark interest among audiences. Even at number one, he was just an aside, a footnote in the story of Tiger.

Tiger and Vijay had always had a cordial, yet chilly relationship. It was clear to everyone around them that the two men simply didn't care for each other, but there were never any fireworks, no excitement or passion in their rivalry. When they did speak, the conversations were more awkward than they were unpleasant; the two golfers just didn't have much to say to each other. Tiger wasn't even exceptional in this regard: Vijay had few friends on the tour. People respected him and his game, and they didn't dislike him, but he just wasn't a popular player. He was the kind of player who would shake hands with his competitors and return to his home and family. He wasn't the type to have a drink with the guys at the clubhouse bar.

This detachment made Vijay an unsuitable rival for Tiger, and the PGA couldn't successfully play them up as adversaries. With little name recognition and a quietly prickly personality, Vijay was branded as boring. The players didn't care about him, the press didn't write about him, and, most importantly, the viewers didn't watch him. Vijay was simply a golfer who had surpassed Tiger for a short time, much the way that horses jockey for position during a race. Vijay would make little impact on the long-term narrative of Tiger's career.

Internally, Tiger's managers were more concerned about the second-place ranking than they would publicly admit. The Tiger brand could withstand just about anything but losing. Tiger received endorsements and sponsorships because he was a winner; corporations wanted to attach themselves to the best players in the world, and Tiger currently didn't qualify. Tiger's team pressured him gently to keep working on his swing, to keep practicing and developing his skill. Doing so was important not only to the game of golf, but also to Tiger's bottom line.

Ernie Els was challenging Tiger for second place, and he briefly succeeded, pushing Tiger down to the number three spot. For any other golfer, it would be part of the natural evolution of the game: There would be periods of wins and losses, none of which would be a cause for concern. But this was Tiger Woods, the man who had been untouchable just a few months earlier, and commentators wondered how long the freefall was going to last.

To say that anyone put pressure on Tiger to win would be an overstatement. Tiger Woods was still a marketable brand, an A-lister in a sport of unknowns. As he worked through his slump, he received encouragement from everyone around him: his caddy, his agents, and, most of all, Earl Woods. Earl's health wasn't great—he would never be mistaken for a young man again—but he was now able to travel with Tiger to tournaments, where he would watch his son with a mixture of pride and concern, his hand stroking his face nervously.

Other people were worried about Tiger, but Earl had the peace that comes with the belief that everything Tiger did was preordained, that his wins and losses were fated by a higher power, and that all Tiger needed to do was to be faithful in his practice. "I tried not to put pressure on him," Earl would say. "He didn't need my pressure; he needed my support. Tiger doesn't respond to being badgered, but he responds to being encouraged and loved."

For his part, Tiger found the slump unsettling; his identity was as the world's best golfer. If he wasn't the best player in the world, who was he? "I won't lie," he would say later. "Nobody likes losing. I don't like losing. I was a little bit worried, even though I knew I would come back. I didn't know how long this was going to go on, and that was what made me nervous. I would have rounds that went well, followed by rounds that were horrible. I needed to develop consistency with my new swing; that was tough to do. But I knew I'd come back, eventually. I didn't know when."

Whatever the worries about his game, Tiger had other matters to think about. Things were changing in his personal life. For the first time since he had gone pro, his golf career wasn't his top priority.

CHAPTER 9

ELIN NORDEGREN WAS NOT THE TYPE of young woman to date Tiger Woods, at least not at first. For one thing, she had a boyfriend at home in Sweden. He was a normal, decent guy, driving a forklift in a warehouse in Skellefteå. If things worked out with him, her life would be safe and predictable, an option that Elin actually found extremely appealing. Dating Tiger Woods would be just the opposite: Paparazzi and tabloids would be around every corner, and Elin couldn't bear the thought of such an invasion of privacy. Besides, she really didn't find Tiger attractive; he simply wasn't her type.

Elin never planned to marry an American; she had come to the States on a whim and certainly didn't plan to stay for long. After graduating from Danderyds High School in northern Stockholm, Elin was accepted into the psychology program at Lund, one of Sweden's most prestigious universities. To make ends meet, she did some cheesecake modeling before taking a job at Champagne, an upscale clothing store in the small town of Täby, about twelve miles north of Stockholm. Efficient and pleasant, Elin caught the eye of several customers, including Mia Parnevik, the wife of pro golfer Jesper Parnevik. Mia was looking for a nanny for her two children in America and asked

Elin if she'd be interested. To her own surprise, Elin accepted, and she quickly moved to Florida to live with the family. Almost immediately, single golfers started hanging around the house, including a very interested Tiger Woods.

The first time he asked her out, in November 2001, Tiger suggested that they grab dinner and a movie. Elin declined, citing a previous obligation. In reality, she didn't have plans for that night; she just didn't want to go out with him. Tiger was stunned; he hadn't been rejected since becoming famous, and Elin's lack of interest brought back distant memories of his previous strikeouts with girls. He had thought fame would insulate him from rejection, but he quickly learned that fame could magnify it. If a woman turned him down despite his fame and riches, she must really dislike him.

He pulled Jesper Parnevik aside and asked him about Elin. Who was she, and did she have a boyfriend? Laughingly, Jesper told Tiger that he could keep trying, but Elin would probably never be interested. He just wasn't her type.

The challenge of the pursuit appealed to Tiger, and he started to visit the Parneviks' house frequently, always making it a point to flirt with Elin and ask her for a date. The more Elin declined, the more insistent Tiger became. He wanted her—no, he needed her—to go on a date with him. On his fifth request, Elin finally agreed to go out with him, but only for one date. She had just ended things with her boyfriend and thought that an evening with Tiger Woods might actually be fun. Besides, she knew he would keep asking her out until she said yes, so perhaps this was the easiest way to get him off her back.

She thought he would try to impress her, to ostentatiously show off his wealth. She had heard stories of his high-flying life, and she wondered if he would make a grand gesture to win her affections. She hoped not; she found displays of wealth gauche, a sign of insecurity. The quickest way to turn Elin off would be to try to dazzle her with his money.

The evening was nothing remarkable, and it was nothing like Elin expected. Tiger arrived at the Parneviks' house in his Jeep and drove her to a nearby restaurant. It was a pleasant enough date; the conversation flowed freely, and for the first time Elin decided that she found Tiger cute and charming. Dinner was followed by a movie—a forgettable romantic comedy that was just right for a first date. Although she would tell friends that she had a nice time, she had some nagging doubts about entering a serious relationship with some-one on the level of Tiger Woods. She was fresh from a breakup and wasn't sure she wanted to start dating again. She also didn't want people to think she was a gold digger, and she wasn't really inter-ested in being famous. She would prefer to live her life in anonymity, an option she wouldn't have if she continued to go out with Tiger.

Elin had also heard rumors about Tiger. He was one of the first golfers with real groupies, and she knew that he enjoyed the attention of pretty girls. He was only twenty-six, and she doubted he was ready for a serious relationship. Why would one of the world's most eligible bachelors settle down with one girl when he could be having sex with as many women as he wanted? She doubted there would be a second date, and that was fine with her. Besides, wasn't he still dating Joanna Jagoda? Elin didn't want to get caught up in the drama of someone else's breakup.

As it turned out, Tiger and Joanna were living separate lives by the time he asked Elin out. Their relationship was cooling just as Elin and her boyfriend were breaking up. Both Tiger and Elin were unattached, although not free of the baggage of recent breakups.

A week later, Tiger called Elin and asked her to dinner. Almost without meaning to, Elin accepted, and before she knew it, she was having dinner with him at the Ale House, a sports bar near the Parneviks' house. Tiger and Elin spent the evening talking about their friends and family, comparing notes on their very different childhoods. For the first time, Elin didn't feel that she was with a celebrity; she felt that she was out with a nice, normal guy. He reminded her of her old boyfriend, albeit a rich, American version of him. She was surprised to be falling for him so quickly.

To everyone around them, Tiger Woods and Elin Nordegren seemed as different as two people could possibly be. She was a homebody; he stayed out late and partied until dawn. She was content with very little; he was a conqueror, constantly searching for the next challenge. She was genuine, polite, and engaging; he was withdrawn and introspective, often being perceived as rude to those around him.

And there was the racial difference. Even though Tiger and Elin made no issue of their diverse backgrounds, some of the conservative members of Isleworth Country Club weren't as color-blind, making snide comments behind the couple's back. Shortly after Tiger started dating Elin, he overheard two members talking in the Isleworth clubhouse. "I don't get it," one golfer said to the other. "Why can't he date a black woman?" They froze as they realized that Tiger had overheard their comments. Enraged, the golfer took a step toward them, his brow furrowed in anger. He then stopped, cocked his head, and sighed, slowly turning away.

The racial issue didn't go away; some members of the black community felt alienated by Tiger's choice to date a white woman. White supremacist groups spewed hatred from their Web sites. Tiger received death threats from anonymous sources.

Elin read some of the press and found it alarming. She made a decision to avoid reading any more stories about her and Tiger; it was a private relationship, and she didn't want to see it played out in public.

Tiger became belligerently defensive about the racial issue. His interracial relationships had never been an issue before. He had dated a blonde girl in Southern California during the Rodney King incident, and he hadn't received nearly the flak that he was receiving now, nine years later. He had never received any flak for dating Joanna; why should it be different now? Perhaps the rules had changed; now that he was an icon, did he have to govern his life differently? Were the expectations different for him now that he was a superstar?

Despite many differences, Tiger and Elin were more alike than anyone could possibly know. They shared a dry sense of humor that allowed them to be sarcastic and cutting with each other, yet each had a thick enough skin to never take the banter personally. They were both competitive, loudly and aggressively sparring in everything from video games to pingpong. They made each other laugh, which was important to Elin. Suddenly, surprisingly, they were in love.

She would tell friends that he made her feel safe, reassuring her of his commitment with loving words and thoughtful gestures. He would say she made him feel comfortable, allowing him to be himself for the first time in years. With her, he wasn't Tiger Woods the golfer; he was a regular guy with a pretty girlfriend. The normalcy of their relationship was appealing to both of them; they settled into a contented courtship full of parties, events, and quiet evenings at home. They became so consumed with each other that she learned to avoid the constant cameras and flashbulbs that were part of the Tiger Woods package. Let them gawk, she decided. She could ignore them.

It was harder, though, for Elin to ignore the women who blatantly flirted with Tiger, even when she was sitting next to him. They would show their cleavage and arch their backs, preening and giggling to get his attention. She grew tired of women who pretended to be absentmindedly sexy, licking their lips and tossing their hair with enough nonchalance to infuse the advances with deniability. It was sickening to Elin, who complained to friends that these women thought of her as an invisible object, a minor annoyance that stood in their way. These women infuriated Elin with their opportunism, and she did her best to ignore them. After all, she didn't want to come across as a jealous girlfriend, even if she occasionally was.

Sometimes, Elin would watch Tiger respond to these women, half flattered and half embarrassed at the attention. He would blush and put his head slightly down, looking at them with sheepish eyes. Even Elin had to admit that he was adorable when he did that, and she noticed that these women thought so as well.

All the while, Elin did have doubts about her new boyfriend's faithfulness. He was traveling nearly nine months out of the year. Could she really trust him to be monogamous? Perhaps that would be too much to ask. She had heard the stories of Tiger's libido from mutual friends. They spoke of his furtive trysts with pretty women, mostly blonde, who seemed to have no other ambition than to bed a famous athlete. His steady stream of hot women was a lively topic within Tiger's circle, and she wondered if she was really something different or just the flavor of the month. She shared some of her fears with her close friends, but largely kept her insecurities to herself.

She wasn't insecure about her looks, however; Elin knew that she was an attractive woman who could turn heads. Her insecurities ran deeper. Was the man she loved able to be faithful to her? And if he wasn't, what would that say about her? She eventually put these fears out of her mind. After all, she had no reason to believe that he was cheating on her. His relationship with Joanna had wound down; he was now a single man. If she had the slightest inkling that he was living a double life, she would be out of there, famous golfer or not.

THEY WEREN'T PICTURES OF ELIN; it was obvious to anyone who knew her. The jawline was different, the eyes were farther apart, and the shy smile was totally wrong. But the naked pictures of the mystery woman started circulating on the Web in 2002 with the caption "Elin Nordegren naked."

In reality, the pictures were of Kim Hiott, a model whose pictures had appeared in a special 2000 issue of *Playboy*. To anyone who didn't know either woman, they shared a passing resemblance, a superficial quality that included hair color and body type.

People wanted to believe the photos were of Elin. During her modeling days, she had posed in some racy bikini shots; it wasn't too much of a stretch to believe the pictures on the Internet were of her. Elin started receiving phone calls from friends who hadn't seen the pictures, asking her why she was posing naked.

It bothered Tiger that people made things up about Elin, especially rumors like this. It was one thing to concoct stories about him; he had chosen the very public life of a professional athlete. But Elin had no desire to become a public figure, and the invasion of her privacy was distasteful to both of them. To neutralize the rumors, Tiger posted a statement on his Web site. "Apparently, some nude photos are making the rounds on the Internet that some claim are of my girlfriend, Elin Nordegren," he wrote. "Although she has done some swimsuit modeling, she has never posed nude, nor does she have any intent to do so."

Elin's glamorous new life was a departure for her. The money and glitz were a stark contrast from her middle-class upbringing. Her father, Thomas Nordegren, a prominent journalist, had once served as Washington, DC, bureau chief for Swedish radio. Her mother, Barbro Holmberg, was a Swedish politician who held several elected positions in local politics. The family had been financially comfortable, but this new ostentatious lifestyle was foreign to Elin.

Not that she was complaining. Her parents had divorced when she was just six, and she alternated her time between two homes. Her mother bought a small townhouse in Vaxholm, where Elin shared a small room with her twin sister, Josefin, and a golden retriever named Lisen. Her older brother, Axel, also lived in the tight quarters. Barbro Holmberg was very socially engaged, even taking in a developmentally disabled teenager to live with the family. It was a cramped home, often cluttered, messy, and noisy, but Elin preferred it to her father's more spacious house.

In any other situation, Elin would have been out of Tiger's league. She was the type of girl he had unsuccessfully pursued as a teenager, the ones who relegated him to the best friend role. She had a lot in common with his high school girl-friend, Dina, a classic blonde beauty with a per-fect bikini body and straight white teeth. Other times, she reminded him of Joanna, a serious woman whose looks belied her intelligence. Tiger desperately wanted Elin on his arm at all his public events. He asked her to quit working for the Parneviks and move into his Orlando home.

In November 2003, Tiger took Elin and some friends to South Africa to watch him play in the Presidents Cup. After spending a day on safari, Tiger invited Elin for a private sunset walk through the 60,000-acre Shamwari Game Reserve. While watching a herd of giraffe running across the plain, Tiger turned to Elin. "I love you," he said to her simply. "I want to spend the rest of my life with you. Elin Nordegren, will you marry me?" He slipped a large solitaire diamond ring on her finger. Surprised, Elin looked at the ring and then looked at Tiger. She started to cry.

"Yes," she sobbed, "oh, yes," before kissing him on the lips. They went back to the lodge and told their friends the good news but warned them not to tell anyone; Tiger and Elin hadn't yet told their parents the happy news and didn't want the word to get out. And they were in South Africa, miles away from the nearest paparazzi. Who would ever find out about the engagement?

Two days later, when the newly betrothed couple arrived at the airport to fly back to the States, a local mayor surprised Tiger by congratulating him on the engagement. A local newspaper had run the story of the proposal, and the report quickly spread around the world. Tiger was livid.

He mentally went through the list of people who knew about the engagement and realized that the only person who could have leaked the news was the founder of the Shamwari Game Reserve. Tiger quickly issued an angry statement:

I thoroughly enjoyed my trip to South Africa for the Presidents Cup, with one exception: I was betrayed by Adrian Gardiner, founder of the Shamwari Game Reserve. He promised to protect my privacy during a four-day stay with friends, but went back on his word, not only alerting the newspapers about my engagement to Elin Nordegren, but inviting the mayor and local school children to the airport when we departed.

Even worse, he took pictures at the reserve to promote his website, and had us detained in a holding cell at the airport so we would pose for more photos with the mayor. Saying we were uncomfortable and totally shocked is an understatement.

In a word, I'm disgusted about the way he handled things. I had been planning to ask Elin to marry me for months and wanted to do it in a private, unique atmosphere. It was such a great moment in our lives, and he cheapened the experience because he was so self-serving. Needless to say, we will never go back.

At the airport, the mayor is saying congratulations, and I haven't even told my parents about the engagement. I really wanted to talk to them about it before the news got out, but it was too late. For a place that supposedly prides itself on privacy, they totally let us down. The only positive out of the whole trip is that Elin didn't say no.

It was a harshly worded missive, and Adrian Gardiner took exception to its angry tone. He released a statement of his own, denying that he had leaked anything to the press, and claiming that the PGA had issued an itinerary of Tiger's vacation to reporters. "The media was actually asked to leave the property," Gardiner said in the statement. "Additional security at all entrances to Shamwari was enforced to keep the media at bay. The Woodses' party was afforded the highest level of privacy."

The controversy blew over in a few days, but the lesson was clear: Tiger Woods treasured his seclusion and would fiercely protect his privacy from anyone who ventured too close to his personal life.

"CAN I TAKE YOUR ORDER?" The pretty waitress at the Orlando Ale House, excited to have a celebrity in her section on a busy Thursday night in early 2004, approached the table where Tiger and Elin were sitting.

"Um, we need a minute," Tiger told her, reaching across the table to hold Elin's hand.

"That's cute," thought the waitress as she walked away. She had heard that Tiger had gotten engaged; the woman he was with was certainly pretty.

Guests at the restaurant craned their heads to look at Tiger and Elin. If they were annoyed by the gawkers, they didn't show it. They stared into each other's eyes as they talked and smiled, still holding hands across the table.

Ten minutes later, the waitress approached the table. "Do you know what you'd like?" she asked. "Do you have any questions about the menu?"

"We haven't even looked at it," Tiger said to her with a smile before turning back to Elin. "Give us a few more minutes."

And so it went for nearly an hour, as Tiger and Elin sat at a corner table at a midpriced chain restaurant in Orlando. Each time the waitress approached, she was reset like an alarm's snooze button, asked to come back in ten minutes. All the while, Tiger and Elin never stopped holding hands.

They finally ordered and picked at their food while they talked. Their meal was a distraction, a diversion from their long conversation.

The dining room started to clear out as the dinner hour ended. Tiger and Elin continued talking, ignoring everyone around them as their food cooled off.

They had spent all evening at the restaurant, ignoring everyone but each other, talking happily the whole time. Tiger had turned his legendary focus onto Elin; for the four hours they sat in the restaurant, she had his full attention.

"All I could think," said the waitress, "was that they had a lot to talk about."

ELIN AND TIGER SETTLED into their new roles as people engaged to be married. Discussions grew more serious. Would they have children? How soon after the marriage? Was divorce an option? What about a prenup? Each question was discussed matter-of-factly but not dispassionately. Tiger and Elin agreed that they would wait a few years to have children, instead enjoying the freedom of being a newlywed couple. Tiger wanted two children: a boy, then a girl. He had always liked the idea of a girl having a big brother to protect her. One thing was definite: Tiger did not want to have only one child. "I would rather have no children than one child," he said. "But in a perfect world, I'd really like to have two kids."

The subject of divorce was more contentious. Elin had felt displaced by her parents' divorce, feeling that she lacked a permanent place in the family. The split had taken a toll on her affections, and she found herself very close to her mother but distant from her father. It was a source of great sadness to Elin, and she talked about it with Tiger, who assured her that their marriage would last.

About a month before the wedding, Elin was presented with a prenuptial agreement. Elin wasn't a fan of these documents—she told friends that it was like setting up the marriage to fail—but she understood why a celebrity like Tiger would have to protect his assets. She looked over the terms and thought they were very fair—generous, even. Elin would be given $20 million if she remained married to Tiger for ten years; that amount would be prorated on a sliding scale depending on the number of years they had been married in the case of an early divorce. If they had children at the time of divorce, an unspecified amount would be paid in child support for each child. The agreement could be renegotiated in extreme circumstances, such as infidelity or abuse. Elin looked over the document and decided to sign it. After all, she loved Tiger; she expected to stay married to him. Besides, she wasn't marrying him to get rich; she was in love.

Tiger gave Elin his calendar and told her to schedule the wedding for a week that he was free. She chose October 5, 2004, a Tuesday. Tiger liked the idea of a weekday wedding: It was so random a date that the paparazzi probably wouldn't figure it out. The gossip magazines went to press on Mondays, so they probably wouldn't be interested in covering the ceremony. Even if they did, they wouldn't be able to get anything on film; the wedding was to be held at Sandy Lane, a private, exclusive resort in Barbados. The newlyweds would honeymoon off the coast of

Barbados in his 155-foot, $22 million yacht, aptly named "Privacy."

Money can buy a lot of things, and Tiger used it to buy solitude and privacy for his wedding. He rented all the rooms at Sandy Lane and two adjoining properties. The wedding would take place in a white tent on a hillside overlooking the ocean. To guarantee privacy, Tiger rented every helicopter on the island and ordered that they be grounded for the day. The paparazzi wouldn't even get close to the wedding.

At sunrise on October 5, 2004, Tiger Woods and two friends woke early and went out on his boat. They spent the morning snorkeling and diving, eating a big breakfast, and talking about golf. In the afternoon, he shaved, then slipped into a beige suit and white shirt. After combing his hair, he was ready.

The preparations were decidedly different in Elin's hotel suite. A bustle of activity surrounded Elin as she applied her makeup while a hair-dresser brushed out her blonde tresses. Brides-maids dressed in sea-foam-green gowns came and went, while Elin's mother took pictures.

Outside, reporters and paparazzi gathered on the terrace of a nearby home. They could see the tent, but a row of strategically transplanted trees kept them from getting a view of the entrance, or of the famous guests as they arrived.

An hour before the ceremony was to begin, the

guests started to arrive. Earl Woods was the first one in the tent, beaming with pride and making small talk with the waiters. As guests arrived, they were checked against a master list and shown to their seats: Charles Barkley and Michael Jordan sat together in the second row, next to two empty seats reserved for no-show Oprah Winfrey. Elin's family arrived shortly thereafter, taking seats in the front row. Kultida Woods was the last to arrive.

Earl had given his blessing to the wedding, but there were still some lingering doubts in his mind. It wasn't that there was anything wrong with Elin—in fact, Earl had grown to love her as a daughter—but the wedding was happening at an inopportune time. Tiger was still slumping on the golf course; he hadn't yet come back to his earlier form since changing his swing, and now he would have to adjust to life as a married man. Earl hoped that Tiger wouldn't let his game fall too far; he still had to make a living, and it would damage his reputation if he didn't quickly bounce back to dominance.

As ceremonies go, the marriage between Tiger and Elin was elegantly simple. Elin, dressed in a white sleeveless floor-length gown, walked down the aisle to the traditional wedding march. Vows were read, rings were exchanged, and each of them promised to stay true until death parted them. Kultida, always a paragon of stoicism and detachment, dabbed at her eyes with a handkerchief as Tiger and Elin kissed for the first time as husband and wife. With beaming faces, they were presented to an applauding audience.

The solemn ceremony soon gave way to a raucous reception. Hootie and the Blowfish—a band approximately ten years past its prime but one of Tiger's favorite groups—performed two sets as guests dined on $300 plates of beef tips, fish, and shrimp. A DJ then took the stage and played dance hits from the 1980s and 1990s as guests ordered cocktails from the open bar. Tiger had several drinks; Elin had none. By the time the $75,000 fireworks display lit up the darkened Barbadian sky, Tiger and Elin had chatted with each wedding guest, with the slightly tipsy golfer telling many people, "I'm the luckiest man in the fucking world."

Marrying Tiger didn't change Elin, except for making her slightly more reserved, less trusting, and less sure of who her friends were. On the PGA Tour, she would keep the other players' wives at arm's length, refusing to get too close. Instead of socializing, a common pastime of golfers' wives, she would solitarily critique her husband's game. Players' wives observed her walking the course as Tiger played, saying very little and focusing on her husband's game. She would walk several steps ahead of him to make sure she got the right view. When other wives approached her, she remained politely aloof, neither rudely dismissing nor enthusiastically embracing them.

Some golfers' wives were offended at Elin's coolness. She soon was given the nickname "Ice Queen" among some of the women, although they were always pleasant to her face. It wasn't that they didn't like Elin; they just thought she didn't like them. Besides, she was so much younger than all of them. What could they possibly have in common?

As the couple celebrated the first few months of marriage, Tiger made fewer public appearances, choosing instead to spend some quiet weeks in their eight-bedroom Orlando home. Elin sat and watched Tiger play video games for hours on end; she loved being with him, and she loved watching him have fun.

Marriage hadn't changed Tiger's appetite for sex, and he was always on the prowl for women. "To put it bluntly, Tiger liked sex," says a television production source. "And I got the feeling that he really liked the pursuit of women. He dated a lot of girls even after he was married to Elin. When he was filming some commercials at Universal Studios, he asked out a few girls, and this was after he was married. If they said no, he'd move on."

Most of the girls Tiger approached were flattered, even if they declined to sleep with him. "I never got the feeling that any of his advances were unwelcome," says the production source, "but I do think they might have been inappropriate sometimes."

Despite the affairs, Tiger maintained that he loved Elin greatly. "He would be flirting with girls all day," says the source, "and then he'd be talking about how happy he was with Elin. I really think he was able to compartmentalize his behavior. He didn't seem to think that his affairs had anything to do with his love for Elin, and vice versa."

With his new responsibilities as a husband and his full schedule of commercials and video games, Tiger started to neglect his golf game. His days of dominance on the course seemed behind him, and sportswriters wondered if they'd ever see the Tiger Woods whom they had grown to admire; he just seemed so uninspired, so unmotivated. The golf world held its breath for a Tiger Woods win; the sport desperately needed it. A resurgent Tiger Woods would be good for both television ratings and revenue.

By January 2005, Tiger was back to playing his full tournament schedule. He still wasn't back to top form, but he won a few tournaments and briefly reclaimed the number one spot in the world, only to be quickly displaced by Vijay Singh. Sponsors were growing nervous, but at least Tiger was playing the game. As he worked, he longed for his home and his wife, and he hoped their relationship would last forever.

It was a happy time for Tiger and Elin, who spent their days hanging out with friends, watching movies, and playing video games. They had settled down into the roles of husband and wife, only to find that they weren't much different from their previous roles as engaged lovers. Tiger would surprise her with lavish, yet thoughtful gifts. Elin would write him love notes and leave them around the house. They were a stereotypical newlywed couple, with stars in their eyes and dreams of a long marriage. This would be their happily ever after, a life full of happiness and promise.

"I love the idea of growing old together," Tiger told *People* magazine that month. "I want to have a relationship where we can change for the better and continue to get closer. It's great when you see people who've been married for 20, 30, 40 years and they're still in love. That's what I want for us."

CHAPTER 10

EARL WOODS'S DEATH didn't come as a surprise to anyone. Even the most casual observer could see that his health was rapidly deteriorating when, in March 2006, he was unable to travel to Ponte Vedra Beach, Florida, to see Tiger in the Players Championship. Earl was usually by Tiger's side at these tournaments, observing his son with a mixture of pride and expectation. Tiger didn't actually have to see Earl to feel his presence; just knowing he was there was enough. Earl was Tiger's muse, the only person on earth who had both the ability and desire to motivate Tiger to greatness.

But Earl wasn't there this time, and his absence was more than conspicuous; it was a palpable, dark feeling that overshadowed everything else. Something was missing, and the tournament just didn't feel right to anyone—not to the people in the gallery, not to the other players, and certainly not to Tiger. Earl had missed tournaments before, but this time was different. Tiger seemed to instinctively know that his father was nearing death; golf was the last thing on Tiger's mind. He wearily managed a smile at the gallery of expectant fans, but it was obvious to everyone that his thoughts were 2,400 miles away in Cypress, California, where Earl lay slowly dying in the master bedroom of Tiger's childhood home.

It wasn't supposed to happen like this; not in this way and certainly not in 2006. From the time Tiger was young, Earl had always told him that he planned to die at age eighty-four. There was no rhyme or reason behind the number; it was simply an age that Earl had arbitrarily chosen. It just sounded like a good age to die: old enough to have a full life, but not necessarily old enough to become a burden. For years, Tiger and Earl operated on the assumption that Earl's prediction would come true; he would pass from this world sometime in 2016, preferably in his sleep. Earl seemed to have a knack for successfully predicting the future; there was no reason to doubt him this time.

But by the time Earl's seventy-fourth birthday rolled around on March 5, 2006, both father and son knew that another decade of life just wasn't going to happen, or if it did, the quality of life would be so compromised that Earl would lose the will to live. The previous twenty years had been rough on his body: He had his first heart bypass surgery in 1986 and a quadruple bypass eleven years later. As he recovered from the second bypass, doctors hit him with another bombshell: He had prostate cancer and would need treatment immediately. In 1998, he started radiation treatment that would further traumatize his body as it successfully shrunk the tumor.

But the cancer was unwilling to stay away, and a recurrence ravished his body with a fierce intensity that stunned everyone around him. Lesions formed on his back, making it uncomfortable for Earl to lie down. A tumor formed behind his eye and steadily grew, often crippling Earl with excruciating headaches. His fight to live outweighed his need for comfort, and he once again subjected his frail body to the excruciating radiation treatments, which again shrunk the tumor at the expense of his immune system. It wasn't just that Earl was dying; he was dying slowly and painfully, precisely the opposite of how he had always expected to die.

Even as his body was shutting down, Earl's mind was sharp and focused, and he could occasionally conjure enough energy to tell his familiar tales to the nurses and doctors who surrounded him. He especially delighted in telling them about a near-death experience he had gone through after his second heart surgery. While recovering in the hospital, Earl's blood pressure had dropped precipitously as his heart rate flat-lined, rendering him clinically dead. As Tiger and Kultida called a nurse for help, Earl had the stereotypical near-death experience: floating along a long tunnel, seeing a bright light at the end, and feeling an overwhelming peace. He would have been perfectly happy to die—he thought of it as a peaceful transition to the next life—but a nurse gave him a shot of adrenaline, jolting his heart back into compliance and restarting the steady cadence of his pulse. The out-of-body incident became an epiphany for Earl, who then claimed to no longer fear death. He now thought of it as a natural part of life, and he'd let go when the time came.

In late March, Earl's prognosis was dire and his health was steadily deteriorating. Decades of inactivity and junk food had finally caught up with Earl, and his faltering heart was leaving him exhausted and immobile, unable to sit up, let alone get out of bed. And then there were the cigarettes. Earl's two-pack-a-day addiction to tobacco was legendary; he had started smoking fifty years earlier while in the army, and despite some halfhearted attempts to quit, he smoked heavily for the rest of his life. The cigarettes were ubiquitous; everyone who knew Earl was used to seeing him with a lit one in his hand. It was a habit that Tiger despised, and he persistently, and unsuccessfully, badgered his father to stop smoking or at least cut back.

As Earl Woods continued to wind down, Tiger spent more time in Cypress, sleeping in his childhood bedroom and checking on his father throughout the night. They didn't discuss the inevitability of death; they both knew that Earl was dying, and it didn't seem to make much sense to keep talking about it. Besides, Tiger knew everything he needed to know about his father's condition: Death was evident in his voice, in the way he moved. It was in his eyes.

The last thing Tiger wanted to do was to play golf; it seemed so trivial to win yet another tournament while Earl languished at home. Tiger wanted to spend time with his father, if just to sit by his bed and watch him sleep. He proposed taking some time off to Earl; perhaps Tiger could skip a few tournaments to spend some extra time at home.

Earl didn't like the idea; he had never been a burden before, and he wasn't about to become one now. "I don't need to be treated like an invalid," Earl told Tiger. "Just go play golf."

Tiger flew to Ponte Vedra Beach for the Player's Championship, but immediately had second thoughts about his decision to leave Earl. His life was ebbing away, and Tiger feared leaving his father for any reason. During the final practice round, the regret continued to grip Tiger, so he left the course and took a private jet across the country to spend time with Earl. He walked through the doors of his childhood home in Cypress, expecting a heartfelt reunion.

Earl looked up sharply as Tiger entered the room. "Tiger," he said with an arched eyebrow. "What the hell are you doing here?"

"I came to see you, Pop," Tiger replied.

Earl sighed loudly. "Get your ass back to Florida."

Tiger didn't even bother to argue with his father; it would just expend too much energy, and he'd end up losing the fight anyway. Earl had definite opinions about how things should be, and obedience was usually the path of least resistance. It was always easier to do Earl's bidding than to oppose him; especially now, Earl needed to be humored. Reluctantly but obediently, Tiger boarded his jet and returned to the Player's Championship with high hopes of winning the tournament in Earl's honor.

But Tiger's mind and, more importantly, his heart weren't in the game, and he shot a three-over 75 in the final round to tie for twenty-second place. If there was any consolation for Tiger, it was that he was paired with Darren Clarke, whose wife, Heather, was battling the breast cancer that would claim her life later that summer.

The weather reflected the seriousness of the mood as the two men played under foreboding, sullen gray clouds. The occasional drizzling rain drenched the Stadium Course at the TPC at Sawgrass. They walked the course somberly, speaking in hushed tones about their respective struggles, drawing comfort from each other as they went through the motions of playing the tournament. After it was over, Tiger spoke briefly to the assembled reporters. "There's a chance I might not play for a while," he said. "Who knows? It all depends on how my father is doing."

He knew what was coming; everyone knew. Earl was fading quickly, and although no one knew how long he would last, the inevitable was rapidly approaching. After the Players Championship, Tiger fled to California, sitting quietly with his father and making sure that nothing would be left unsaid. Earl was weak, and the light was fading from his eyes. Tiger would soon be alone.

It was a strange, heartbreaking spring, and as April approached, it became obvious that Earl was holding on until the next Masters, hoping to see Tiger win for a fifth time. Again, Tiger reluctantly boarded a plane, this time flying to Augusta to compete in the tournament that held a special significance to both men. Tiger promised Earl, and himself, that he would play the Masters to the zenith of his ability; it would be a win dedicated to his father. But distraction combined with exhaustion, and Tiger just wasn't able to play his best, finishing in a five-way tie for third place. It was a disappointing loss. Tiger had profoundly and urgently wanted his father to see him wear the green jacket one more time; he knew there would be no other chances. Tiger despondently returned to Cypress to sit with his father one more time while they waited.

As difficult as the time was for Tiger, it was strangely familiar to him. Earl had always had health problems, at least for as long as Tiger could remember, and Tiger had gotten used to the fact that his father was an older man. It wasn't spoken about, at least not much. It was one of those things that they both just understood.

There comes a stage in every parent/child relationship where the roles reverse; the child becomes the adult. The change usually happens organically and subtly, often with neither party recognizing the evolution of the relationship. Earl's failing health accelerated his dependence on his son, making both men painfully aware of the transition. Tiger was now the adult, and he became Earl's conscience, constantly reminding him to eat correctly, exercise regularly, and, most importantly, quit smoking.

Not that Earl Woods would really make the lifestyle changes that Tiger wanted. Earl was a strong-willed man, mulish and immovable, stubbornly doing as he pleased. In 1997, he had lost thirty-five pounds on a low-fat diet, but he quickly packed the weight back on. Earl wasn't going to start taking care of himself—not now, at least—but Tiger would never give up trying to get his father to live healthier; the stakes were just too high.

I'm very saddened to share the news of my father's passing at home early this morning. My dad was my best friend and greatest role model, and I will miss him deeply. I'm overwhelmed when I think of all of the great things he accomplished in his life. He was an amazing dad, coach, mentor, soldier, husband and friend. I wouldn't be where I am today without him, and I'm honored to continue his legacy of sharing and caring. Thank you to all who are sending condolences to my family and our Foundation. We are truly blessed to have so many who care during this difficult time.

This was the worst day of Tiger's life. Even though Earl's death was expected, it was hard for Tiger to comprehend that his father was really gone, that the man behind the world's most famous athlete would never again get to watch his son compete. Tiger got the devastating news on the morning of May 3, 2006, that Earl had died overnight, his heart simply giving out for the last time. As word spread around the golfing community, Tiger's phone started to ring: Competitors and friends wanted to express their sympathies, to mourn the loss with Tiger, to just be there for him. But Tiger didn't want to speak to anyone, at least not at first. His relationship with Earl was something epic, a relationship like none other. He didn't want to talk it out with anyone else; he just wanted to be alone with his thoughts.

There were only two people whom Tiger wanted to see: his mother and his wife. The three of them sat together in Kultida Woods's house, talking about their time with Earl and looking to the future. Of everyone in Earl's life, Tiger was taking the loss the hardest; he was unable to speak about Earl without getting emotional. On the afternoon after Earl's death, he held Kultida and wept while Elin looked on, wiping away her own tears.

Tiger had always coveted his father's praise and acceptance; even after Tiger ascended to super-stardom, Earl's approval was all that Tiger needed. Sure, he needed the accolades of others, but it was

Earl's words of affirmation that truly propelled Tiger. Now Earl was silenced, and Tiger felt more alone than he had ever felt before. He wasn't just a man who had lost a father; he had lost a best friend, coach, cheerleader, and confidant. Tiger would never be the same, and he instantly recognized that his life had changed forever.

There were funeral plans to make, and Tiger and Kultida figured out the best way to honor Earl's legacy. There would be no public service, but a small, intimate gathering in Santa Ana where those closest to Earl could pay their respects. The Friday after his death, the service happened without incident; the media exercised rare restraint, and Tiger was able to say a tearful good-bye away from the camera's glare.

There would be no golf for a few weeks; Tiger refused to pick up a club. The memories were too raw, the pain too great. Golf had been the way for Earl and Tiger to bond, and taking to the links was unthinkable for Tiger, at least while the pain was so fresh. Tiger would return to the sport eventually—sooner than most people expected— as time started the slow, arduous process of healing his wound.

On June 15, just six weeks after losing Earl, Tiger reappeared in public for the first time, at Winged Foot Golf Club, where he played nine holes in preparation for the U.S. Open. It was good to see him back on the course; his presence indicated healing had begun. The media followed his every step, waiting to hear what he would say. When the assembled reporters learned that Tiger would speak at a press conference, they quickly jockeyed for position, scrambling to hear his first public comments since his life's irrevocable change.

Tiger was not one to burst into tears—at least not in public—so if any reporters had been hoping for a show of raw emotion, they were disappointed. Tiger spoke precisely and deliberately, with his unwavering voice reflecting on his father's legacy. His focus was oddly appropriate; his respectful comments became a fitting tribute for the man who had taught Tiger the art of stoicism and focus. There were occasional glimpses of pain in his eyes, but everything—his words, his body language, his mannerisms—showed the restraint and self possession that had made him so unknowable to the public.

In the end, it may have been the most candid Tiger would ever be in a press conference. "I really had no desire to get back to the game of golf," he confessed. "I think one of the hardest things for me, in all honesty, was to get back to the game of golf, because a lot of my memories, great memories that I have with my dad, are at the golf course.

"It was hard at times going out there late in the evening like I always do to practice," he said, "and I remember starting back—anytime you take time off and start back, you always work on your fundamentals: grip, posture, stance, alignment. Well, that's what I learned from Dad."

When he addressed his decision to get back on the golf course so quickly after Earl's death, his voice became intensely quiet, a window into Tiger's introspective grief. "It was certainly a little more difficult than I expected," he said, his eyes clear. "But also, then again, it brought back so many great memories, and every time I thought back I always had a smile on my face. As I was grinding and getting ready, it was also one of the great times, too, to remember and think back on all the lessons, life lessons Dad taught me through the game of golf. All these things come rushing back to you."

A reporter raised his hand and asked Tiger how he found the strength to move forward from his grief. What was the one thing that kept him going during this time of mourning?

"The overwhelming support, the letters and the e-mails and the phone calls, really shocked me," Tiger replied. "I was very surprised. All the companies that I work with, the people that I haven't talked to in years called. It really was eye-opening. It made this time in my life, and my mom's and all the friends that my dad knew and had, it made it a lot easier. It really did."

Another reporter asked Tiger to remember his father as a coach. Was there a special gift he had?

"Love," Tiger replied quickly, without missing a beat. "That's basically it. The love that we shared for one another and the respect that we had for one another was something that's pretty special."

Tiger didn't want to come back to golf until he could apply his acute concentration to his game, ignoring all of life's distractions as he played. He hoped that six weeks would be a long enough hiatus; he could come back and win one for Earl. He thought that he was thinking clearly, that he had quickly and efficiently bounced back from his grief.

As he started the first round, a man in the gallery shouted, "God bless your father, Tiger." The words hung in the air for a moment, and Tiger managed a slight smile in response, but he seemed rattled; his legendary focus was gone.

It would be the worst performance in a majors championship of Tiger's career as he vainly tried to regain his focus and concentrate solely on playing the game. The first round came and went, and Tiger posted a 76 on the scoreboard. The second round was equally as dismal, and Tiger once again shot well over par. His two-day total of 152 put him out of the U.S. Open; he wouldn't make the cut for the first time in his career. Onlookers politely ignored Tiger's streams of profanity accompanying each shank; he was clearly in pain, and now was not the time to upbraid him for his temper.

"I'm pissed," he said at the postround press conference. "That pretty much sums it up right there."

Tiger Woods was lost on the golf course, still

adjusting to life without Earl. Players on the tour expressed their concern and encouragement, both to Tiger and to the media. Kultida Woods spent weeks at Tiger's Florida mansion, grieving with Tiger over a man whom she could not live with but deeply loved nonetheless. The fans sent thousands of letters to him, urging him to stay strong and move forward. Everyone seemed to want the best for him, and, more importantly, they just wanted the old Tiger Woods back.

Tiger couldn't contain his emotions. He tried to hold back the tears, to maintain his composure, at least until he could have a good cry in private. He never really liked to wear his feelings on his sleeve, and he hadn't intended to make a display of his tears on July 23. His father had been gone for about ten weeks, and Tiger was now celebrating the first victory that Earl would never see.

He had ferociously dominated the 2006 Open Championship, with his fierce focus evident on nearly every shot—he hit the fairway 92 percent of the time, finishing with three eagles, nineteen birdies, forty-three pars, and seven bogeys. It was one of his most impressive tournaments ever, with his score of eighteen under par just one stroke off his major championship record. It was a game of competence and self-assuredness that electrified the record crowds that enthusiastically cheered every shot. Tiger Woods was back, at least professionally.

As he approached his last putt, his caddie, Steve

Williams, lowered his voice and spoke into his ear. "This one's for Dad," he whispered to Tiger right before the winning putt.

Tiger wasn't known to crumble, but the emotion of the win, coupled with the still-raw feelings of his personal loss, was too much for him. He hugged Steve, bawling unabashedly as he finally allowed his pent-up emotions to be seen by everyone. When he saw Elin, he collapsed into her arms, weeping as his wife wiped her eyes.

In the post-tournament press conference, the first question was about Earl Woods. How would he have reacted to the win?

"He would have been very proud, very proud," Tiger said, flashing a toothy grin reminiscent of a younger, more innocent Tiger Woods. "He was always on my case about thinking my way around the golf course and not letting emotions get the better of you, because it's so very easy to do in this sport. Just use your mind to plot your way around the golf course, and if you had to deviate from the game plan, make sure it's the right decision to do that."

And about the tears? "I've never done that," he sheepishly admitted. "You know me: I guess I'm kind of the one who bottles things up a little bit and moves on, tries to deal with things in my own way. But at the moment it just came pouring out. After the putt, all these emotions just poured out of me. They have been locked in there."

He continued. "I just miss my dad so much. I wish he could have been here to witness this. He enjoyed watching me grind out major wins, and this would have brought a smile to his face."

The Open was just the first of many times that Tiger would rear back after his father's death. Four weeks later, he dominated the PGA Championship, again finishing at eighteen under par. He had shot only three bogeys, tying the record for the fewest in a major. If anything, Earl's death had made Tiger a more fearsome competitor; he now had something greater to play for: his father's legacy.

The Buick Open followed, marking Tiger's fiftieth professional tournament win. He won six consecutive PGA Tour events, showing the world that he had not lost his notorious focus. Rather than being a reasonable excuse for losing, Earl's death was now his motivation to methodically destroy his competitors as he triumphed in a long string of victories.

"TIGER, HAVE YOU EVER CONSIDERED seeing someone about your grief?" The friend meant well, and concern was evident on his face. He hadn't seen any real warning signs, just a general funk that had hovered over Tiger since his father's death. Sure, he was winning golf tournaments, but he was personally acting preoccupied, unhappy, and irritable. He would show up on the golf course wrinkled and unshaven, looking like he had just rolled out of bed. Maybe a grief counselor would do him some good.

"I haven't," said Tiger listlessly. "I haven't had the time."

"Well, I wish you would," the friend replied. "Just a few times, maybe just to talk things over. It doesn't have to be anything big."

"Thanks," Tiger replied with a smile. "I'll keep that in mind."

Whether or not Tiger ever saw someone was a secret that Tiger kept from his closest friends. He played his emotional cards close to the vest; he didn't share his secrets with anyone. But the people around him hoped that Tiger would get better, that he had turned a corner and could find some happiness.

In reality, he was an emotional wreck. The emptiness engulfed him; emotions were raw, and Tiger often found himself breaking down at the littlest things. His grief was more than overwhelming; it was all-consuming. He struggled to right himself, to move forward from his mourning and once again take control of his life. Despite the accolades and achievements, the pretty wife and the millions of dollars, he became unhappy and withdrawn.

HE WAS DANCING with a pretty blonde, a girl who looked strikingly like Elin. The club owner watched him in befuddled amazement. It was so blatant, so obvious. Tiger Woods was in his club, drinking and dancing with a woman who wasn't his wife, and there were no tabloid reporters anywhere. No one was paying attention.

The first call the club owner made was to the local newspaper. This would be good publicity for the club; he wanted to bring in celebrity seekers. He was passed around the news desk of the *Orlando Sentinel,* but no one was interested in the story. When he finally spoke to a sportswriter, he was told that they'd look into it and call him back; they never did.

He called the celebrity magazines: *People, InTouch, Star, Us Weekly.* No one returned his calls, and the one person he spoke with told him that they weren't interested in the story. Frustrated, the club owner sat in the VIP section, watching Tiger grind against the pretty girl until 2:00 a.m. No one cared.

Tiger had had affairs before Earl's death, clandestine and sex-fueled trysts with various women. Some of the women had been long-term affairs; others had lasted for just a few days or just for one night. After Earl's death, Tiger went into overdrive, and he began to take unnecessary and surprising risks in his sex life: picking up women in bars, having unprotected sex, having affairs in his marital bed.

"I never thought he was out of control," explains the television production source who worked with Tiger more than fifty times. "I just thought that he liked to have sex, which isn't really anything shocking for a young athlete. Before all the dirt came out, I think most men would have envied his life, to have so much access to sexy women. You can call it what you want, like an addiction or whatever, but he was living every guy's dream."

When the scandal broke in late 2009, Tiger would be linked to more than a dozen women, most of them claiming to have slept with him during this era. All of them wouldn't be telling the truth, of course, but Tiger's actions during this period would render him unable to plausibly deny any of the allegations.

The tailspin continued throughout 2006, and Tiger seemingly became unable to control his actions; he was living a risky life of sexual addiction, fed not only by his own libido, but also by his unspeakable sadness. He was inconsolable, and he used sex as a medication to fix things.

Tiger wished that he and Elin had had children before Earl died. Sure, it bothered him that Earl wouldn't be around to see him shatter golf records, but Tiger could get past that; after all, his father saw the first decade of his professional career and died knowing that his son was an exceptional player who had changed the game. But Earl was going to miss out on the most rewarding and profound experience of Tiger's life: fatherhood. It pained Tiger to think about this loss.

Tiger had planned to start a family, and he wanted his children to know their grandfather.

Tiger knew that Earl would be great with the kids; he might spoil them a little bit, but he would love being a grandfather. And the children would adore Earl. It would be fun to watch them together.

But it wasn't meant to be; Earl died just four months before Elin became pregnant for the first time. Like many first-time expectant parents, Elin and Tiger kept the pregnancy a secret for the first trimester; there was no sense in telling anyone until they knew that everything was okay. But as the pregnancy progressed, Tiger and Elin started calling everyone to share the good news. Tiger still couldn't believe that Earl was gone; he profoundly wanted to call his father and tell him the news, and the reality of Earl's death was still achingly raw.

Tiger would later say that everything he learned about fatherhood came from Earl. He'd claim that Earl led by example, teaching him how to lead a family through both discipline and love. He still heard Earl's voice on the golf course, but nowhere was his voice louder than when Tiger was interacting with his own children.

Elin went into labor on Father's Day 2007, and they rushed to Winnie Palmer Hospital in Orlando —a hospital started and sponsored by the one man, aside from Earl, whom Tiger looked up to the most, Arnold Palmer. Tiger was an eager participant in his daughter's birth, watching everything in the delivery room, emotion washing over him as he heard her first cry. Holding her in his arms, Tiger named her Sam, after a nickname that his father had for him. She would be known as Sam Alexis Woods.

Tiger had always been a night owl, and he was happy to go through the midnight feedings and diaper changes. Taking time off golf, he planned to enjoy the first few months of his daughter's life. Sam wasn't a sickly child, but she caught a few colds that made her miserable. It was a period of little sleep, but Tiger would later say that it was among the most rewarding periods of his life.

In December, as he prepared for the Target World Challenge tournament, he seemed ready to talk about the previous sixteen months and how they had changed him. He was about to turn thirty-two, and it was clear he was no longer a child, but a man who talked of regrets, sadness, and hope.

"Fatherhood has made me appreciate the little things of life," he told the assembled reporters at the Sherwood Country Club, near Los Angeles. "After my father passed away, I think probably every kid feels the same way I felt, that I didn't spend enough time with him. I certainly felt that way about my dad. I'd call him all the time and I was there as much as I could be but you always feel that you didn't really capture each and every day with him.

"I wanted to feel that I had done that with my daughter," he continued. "I wanted to feel and appreciate that, even during the sleepless nights and the difficulties when she was sick. You still have to appreciate these days because you don't know when they are ever going to end.

"I always thought my dad would live forever," he continued. "I thought he was immortal. Obviously, we all know that's not the case. But I wanted to be sure that I truly appreciated these days with my daughter.

"I think I've grown up a bit this year. After my dad died, I played well but I still wasn't feeling all that great about life in general. When I had Sam this year I wanted to take each moment and appreciate everything. That's where my life has changed."

He paused for a minute. "It's sad," he said softly. "I wish I had been able to realize how good life was when he was here."

TIGER'S ARTHROSCOPIC SURGERY in April 2008 knocked him out of the game for two months, and the subsequent reconstructive surgery removed him from competition for the rest of the 2008 season. Tiger spent much of the time with Elin and Sam, doing all the things that devoted fathers were supposed to do: playing games, singing songs, teaching Sam how to walk and talk. With the attention of both parents, Sam flourished, learning to speak both English and Swedish.

It was a blessing, spending time with his daughter, and Tiger wanted to be a doting dad, to put into use the lessons he had learned from Earl: patience, teaching, and, most importantly, unconditional love. If there was a drawback to his time at home, it was that Tiger had more time than ever to reflect on the loss of Earl. Even though it had been nearly two years since Earl's death, the loss was still acute. Each day was better than the one before, but Tiger's healing process was painfully slow.

The sexual affairs didn't stop during these months, although Tiger's limited travel kept them from happening as frequently. Money gave Tiger many options, and he had affairs with women closer to home: Orlando women whom he'd meet at clubs around central Florida. One of his favorite hangouts was the Blue Martini, a corporate-looking bar attached to an upscale mall. Just a ten-minute drive from Tiger's house, the bar was a visible place for Tiger to be seen; the VIP area was just a few velvet ropes in full view of the rest of the bar. Tiger would meet women there, flirting and hugging them, oblivious—or not caring—that people were watching him. Perhaps he felt that he was above the law, that he could get away with anything, that no one would dare question what he did.

By summer 2007, Elin was pregnant again, less than a year after Sam's birth. The children would be twenty months apart in age, and Tiger hoped for a boy.

On February 8, Elin again went to Winnie

251

Palmer Hospital, this time to give birth to Charlie Axel. It was a surprising name—most people speculated that Tiger might name the boy Earl. Charlie was a name they both liked, and the middle name, Axel, was the first name of Elin's older brother. The name was fitting: In Swedish culture, the name Axel means "my father is peace."

Tiger had always wanted to have two children: a boy first, followed by a girl. It didn't happen the way he had planned, but Tiger didn't care; he had two healthy, happy children, which was all he needed.

"I really can't complain," he said that June. "I have been blessed, more than most people are blessed, and I love being a husband and father. It's who I am."

CHAPTER 11

TIGER WAS STRONGER than he had ever been before, a precision machine ruthlessly dispatching opponents while winning an impressive string of tournaments. If anyone had ever doubted that Tiger Woods was the best golfer in the world, his resurgence put the lie to that doubt. It was more a reclaiming of the top spot, an unmistakable reiteration of his greatness. As Tiger grew comfortable with his new swing—a collaborative effort between him and Hank Haney—he regained his focus and stormed back with a ferocity that stunned everyone in the golf world.

It was good news for the sport; a slumping Tiger was bad for ratings. No one tuned in to watch Tiger lose; everyone wanted to see him win. The slump had affected the PGA Tour television ratings, which had dipped by nearly 20 percent during 2003 and 2004. Conventional wisdom held that Tiger's decline was responsible.

But he was back now, and excitement in the sport was reignited: in advertisers, in golfers, and, most importantly, in the audience. Tiger was a showman, a guy who could electrify a crowd by his mere presence. He didn't even have to try.

Tiger's resurgence had really begun in 2005 when he won the Masters for the fourth time. The victory helped him to wrestle the number one spot away from Vijay Singh in the Official World Golf Rankings. For the next few months, Tiger and Vijay battled for the top spot like boxers, trading jabs as they struggled for dominance. But after his victory at the 2005 Open Championship—his second time winning the tournament and his tenth major championship—Tiger reclaimed the top spot for good. He was the undisputed number one, the heavyweight champ of the golf world. The rest of 2005 was a good year, with Tiger winning six money events on the PGA Tour. It was his best year since his dominating period between 1999 and 2002.

Tiger was still on track to beat Jack Nicklaus's record of eighteen Majors wins. Tiger was twenty-nine years old when he won his tenth championship; Nicklaus had been thirty-two at his tenth. With a few more wins, Tiger would be in striking distance: Nicklaus had notched his last win at the 1986 Masters, when he was forty-six. Not yet thirty, Tiger probably had more than half of his career ahead of him.

At Tiger's level of celebrity, the wins and the losses hadn't translated into any more, or less, money. Although his winnings had dropped in 2003 and 2004, his endorsement payouts continued to mount, dwarfing the money he earned on the PGA Tour. In 2004, he had earned just $6.3 million on the tour, but $83 million in endorsements. Tiger was an A-lister, and it would take more than a two-year slump to knock him off his pedestal as the top-earning athlete in the world. His golf game was almost irrelevant at this point; he had transcended the game, entering into a new echelon of celebrity. He pocketed another $87 million in winnings and endorsements in 2005, followed by nearly $99 million in 2006. Everything was going his way.

THE NAKED PICTURES WERE BACK, and no one was more unhappy about them than Elin Nordegren Woods. For four years, she had been aware of the persistent rumors that she had posed naked, even though it was clear, at least to her, that the pictures were of someone else. The rumors never went away, and they would arise at the most inopportune moments. The pictures were continually reposted on X-rated sites and celebrity blogs, almost always accompanied by lewd comments. Elin ignored the rumors as best she could, but the lies always got under her skin; she didn't understand why people were so fascinated with the idea of seeing Tiger Woods's wife naked.

But this time was different. The photos had escaped the realm of shadowy porn sites and found their way into the mainstream media. *The Dubliner* magazine, a city publication in Ireland's capital, published one of the photos in September 2006. The Ryder Cup was coming to Ireland, and the editors of the magazine thought it would be fun to take aim at the wives of American golfers in a pictorial spread.

The Dubliner claimed that the article was supposed to be a satire, lampooning the ridiculousness of the tabloid media. The accompanying headline described the American golfers' wives as "Ryder Cup Filth." Besides making lewd comments about three other golfers' wives, the story claimed that Elin could be "found in a variety of sweaty poses on porn sites across the web."

Although the publishers maintained that the spread was supposed to be funny, Tiger wasn't laughing. During a pretournament press conference just days after the article had been released, Tiger decided to speak out about it, characterizing the article as an attack on Elin. His comments came as a surprise to many of the assembled media; Tiger usually avoided controversy, so his decision to speak out showed how incensed he was. In front of nearly fifty reporters, Tiger angrily tore into the magazine. His voice was low and intense, but there was no mistaking the fury in his eyes; he was out for blood. "I am very disappointed in how the article was written," he said in measured tones. "Yes, my wife has been a model and she did do some bikini photos, but to link her to porn Web sites is unacceptable. I do not accept it.

"My wife is an extension of me," he continued. "We're in it together. We're a team, and I care about her with all my heart. It's hard to be very diplomatic about this when you have so much emotion involved, when my wife is involved in this."

Tiger wasn't the only one on his team to speak out about the article. When Mark Steinberg spoke to the media, he left open the possibility of a lawsuit, a tactic that seemed to spook the editors. The magazine backed away from the article, insisting that no harm had been meant. One of the editors issued a statement the day after Tiger's comments:

The publishers and staff of *Dubliner* acknowledge that the satirical article was inappropriate and wish to sincerely apologise to Tiger Woods and his wife Elin and other Ryder Cup players and their families for any offence they may have taken to it.

The article was written as a satirical piece and in the context of the entire page the publishers believed that readers would not be left thinking that there was any truth in the assertions, it being an absurd parody of the inaccurate tabloid publishing world generally.

If any contrary impression was given, it certainly was not intended and the publisher unreservedly apologises.

But if the editors were trying to avoid litigation, the apology came too late. Within weeks, Elin had filed a libel suit against *The Dubliner*. A year later, she won a $183,250 settlement from the magazine. In addition to the cash award, the magazine was required to issue several public apologies to Elin, both in the mainstream media and in the next issue. Happy to be vindicated, Elin donated the money to two cancer charities and released a statement of her own, the first time she had ever said anything publicly since meeting Tiger. "The false and deeply offensive article in *The Dubliner* magazine, with the accompanying photograph of another woman wrongly claimed to be me, caused great personal distress to me and my family," she wrote. "We are delighted at today's outcome and relieved that we may now put the experience behind us."

As part of the settlement, *The Dubliner* released a blanket apology and urged the media to disseminate it throughout the world. "The story was cheap, tasteless and deliberately offensive. It was also completely untrue," the statement read. "Ms. Nordegren Woods has never posed, or been photographed, nude. It was a cheap, vulgar lie, which was unforgivably insulting to Ms. Nordegren Woods.

"We now apologise, unreservedly, completely and unequivocally to Ms. Nordegren Woods. We have agreed to pay to her a substantial sum by way of damages." The statement continued: "Ms. Nordegren Woods has, from the outset, expressed her intention to donate the entire sum to a charity of her choice. We recognize and appreciate her generosity in so doing. We should not have discussed Ms. Nordegren Woods at all; we will never do so again."

It was a surprisingly conciliatory statement, almost groveling, and the media could easily see that a warning shot had been fired by Tiger Woods. The message was clear: The media might be able to say what they wanted about Tiger, but if they disparaged Elin Nordegren, Tiger's team would come down on them swiftly and mercilessly.

AS GOOD A YEAR AS 2005 HAD BEEN, 2006 surpassed it, at least in Tiger's professional career. Despite the turmoil in his personal life, Tiger still managed to win eight times on the PGA Tour, again landing him in the top spot on the money board. The slump was a distant memory by now, but Tiger was still dealing with the loss of Earl. He was irritable to his friends and family and acting out sexually, but his game had never been better; his focus was as sharp as it had ever been. Golf continued to be a therapy for him, a way to continue to channel his energies into something productive.

Early in Tiger's career, Earl had said that he communicated with his son telepathically, coaching his game from afar. In true Earl fashion, he would say so with a smirk; his grin would blur the line between joking and seriousness. Reporters had always had a hard time determining if Earl truly believed that he was communicating with his son or if he was just saying so because it sounded good. But Earl said that he and Tiger shared an unspoken bond, and it was just easier to believe that this was true.

After Earl died, it was clear that Tiger continued to feel a bond with him, most keenly on the golf course. As he'd line up his putts, Tiger would move his lips as if he were talking to an unseen companion giving him advice. In press conferences, Tiger said that he and Earl still communicated on the course, and he raised the possibility that Earl's memory was so indelible that Tiger would always hear his father's voice. This idea fit into the Tiger legend nicely: Even death could not sever his bond with his father.

Whatever forces were driving Tiger, whether it was Earl or otherwise, he was playing convincingly. He had never been talkative on the course, but now he was even more introspective, focusing on the game and ignoring every distraction. At the beginning of 2007, Tiger came out swinging with a two-stroke victory at the Buick Invitational, his third consecutive victory there. Shooting fifteen under par, he pocketed $936,000 for the win and started off the year strongly. Tiger was on a roll; he had won the last six tournaments of 2006, and Buick was his lucky number seven.

Although Tiger said that breaking records wasn't his priority, he felt a certain gratification when the records toppled under the weight of his achievements. It was fun to watch the statistics pile up, to hear the pundits speculate about the golfers whom

Tiger was leaving in his wake. The record-breaking became a distraction for Tiger, however, and he refocused on winning each individual tournament rather than on putting all the wins into a broader context of record-breaking. With his third consecutive win at the World Golf Championship in March 2007, Tiger became the first player to have three consecutive victories in five different PGA events.

As winter turned into spring, Tiger prepared for the 2007 Masters tournament. If he won, it would be his fifth Masters win, putting him in second place for total wins behind Jack Nicklaus. Tiger arrived in Augusta to dreary, windy skies and unseasonably cold temperatures. The dismal weather affected everyone's game, not just Tiger's, and he tied for second behind Zach Johnson. He shot three over par, a disappointing result. Tiger knew he could have done better; it just wasn't his year at Augusta.

Later in the summer, Tiger earned his third victory of the season by two strokes at the Wachovia Championship. It was his fifty-seventh win in twenty-four different PGA Tour tournaments. It was ugly, haphazard golf, full of putting mistakes and wild swings. Luck was both for and against Tiger; he had some lucky bounces that turned his bogeys into birdies and some unfortunate blunders that nearly cost him the tournament.

At the following month's U.S. Open, he finished tied for second, the second major of the year in which he ended in second place. A grand slam just wasn't going to happen, at least not in 2007, but Tiger was playing well and winning the majority of his tournaments. Even his losses were close; he would sit near the top of the leaderboard, losing by just a stroke or two. If he could continue to figure out how to eliminate one or two bad shots at crucial moments, there was no reason that he couldn't get a grand slam in 2008.

TIGER HAD ALWAYS BEEN a fast runner; he could run a mile in five minutes. It was his way to blow off steam, to spend time alone with his thoughts. Rain or shine, his neighbors often saw him running around his Isleworth neighborhood, following the same route every day. He was in top physical shape; during the summer, he'd run in a tank top or tight t-shirt, displaying his lean, muscular torso. He was the picture of health, a professional golfer with the build of a track star.

He didn't know what caused the pain; he didn't trip, and there was no debris on the road. It was excruciating, a sharp, throbbing pain that immediately made his knee radiate with heat. Tiger tried to walk the pain off, limping through the neighborhood on his way home.

It turned out that Tiger had torn his anterior cruciate ligament—more commonly known as the ACL—in the same knee that he had previously injured. The pain was intense. It wasn't a dull ache like before; it was a shooting, stabbing pain. Tiger couldn't have surgery now; perhaps after the season was over, he could get the injury taken care of. He again started taking painkillers before each tournament, hoping the pain would subside and he could continue playing.

The painkillers didn't seem to work, at least not at first. His next goal was to win a record-tying third consecutive Open Championship, but he fell out of contention with a second-round 75. After the dismal round, he tried to regain momentum, but he never again mounted a serious charge to victory over the weekend. Although his putting was solid—he sank a ninety-footer in the first round—his iron play held him back. "I wasn't hitting the ball as close as I needed to all week," he said at the post-tournament press conference. He tied for twelfth, five strokes behind the eventual winner, Padraig Harrington. Tiger kept his hurt knee a secret; there was no reason to tell his competitors about his weakness. That was the type of information a competitor keeps to himself, never giving other players an inkling that anything was wrong.

In early August, Tiger continued his strong 2007 by winning his record fourteenth World Golf Championship event, at the Bridgestone Invitational. Bridgestone served as a warm-up for the tournament that really mattered to Tiger: the following week's PGA Championship—one of the four Majors events.

That same month, Tiger stunned everyone by giving an exclusive interview and posing for a photo shoot for *Men's Fitness* magazine, a smaller publication that didn't seem an obvious fit into Tiger's grand marketing strategy. The decision mystified editors of golfing magazines; it just wasn't a logical move, and Tiger was all about logic. No one figured out why Tiger gave the interview; at the time, it never occurred to anyone that *Men's Fitness* was published by American Media, the parent company that also owned the *National Enquirer.* It just never crossed anyone's mind.

THE SUN WAS STILL HIGH above the treeline as the hot August afternoon began to wind down in Manhattan, Kansas. The dark SUV slowly cruised through the large stone gates at Sunset Cemetery, its tires crunching against the gravel driveway. It was a peaceful afternoon, one with little wind and even less noise.

The caretakers were about to leave for the night; the grass had been mowed and the shrubs trimmed. They only half-noticed the vehicle moving along the paved road; people frequently came to the cemetery to visit their loved ones' graves. Sunset Cemetery maintained the grounds and the headstones, but bringing flowers and mementos to the graves was the job of the families.

The SUV door opened, and Tiger stepped out from behind the driver's seat. He walked solitarily and soberly toward the granite gravestone marking Earl's final resting place. Finding the marker, he stood before it, lost in his thoughts as he stood at the spot where his father was buried.

Tiger didn't visit his father's grave often; geography and a busy schedule kept him away. Whenever he visited, he showed up alone, speaking to no one as he stood by the grave to honor his father. It was a place he could be alone with his thoughts; no one approached him as he paid his respects.

There was nothing special about this day; it wasn't an anniversary or a birthday, just a random summer afternoon. The caretakers briefly watched Tiger from a distance—it wasn't every day that they had a superstar visit the cemetery—and then they got in their cars to leave for the day. As they drove off, Tiger was still visiting his father's grave, a solitary man standing silently with his head bowed.

He was in the Midwest for the 2007 PGA Championship, which started later that week in Tulsa. Whether fueled by the graveside visit or by something else, Tiger was a force on the links, braving triple-digit temperatures on every day of the tournament. After a dismal first round, Tiger roared back with a record-tying 63 in the second round; he never lost the lead again and took home the $1.2 million prize. The records continued to pile up: Tiger became the first golfer to win the PGA Championship in back-to-back seasons on two separate occasions. He also became the second golfer after Sam Snead to have won at least five events on the PGA Tour in each of eight different seasons.

As the 2007 season ended, Tiger finished with a runaway victory at the Tour Championship to capture his fourth title in five years. He became the only two-time winner of the event and the champion of the inaugural FedEx Cup, the PGA's first tournament to implement a playoff system. The year had been a good one, both professionally and personally. One thing was clear to everyone: Despite the previous year's loss of Earl, Tiger had managed to find his rhythm as a man without his father.

HE WAS HOBBLING, limping everywhere he went. For several months, he didn't want to believe that, despite his new swing and careful treatment, the pain just wasn't going away. He knew he would have to get something done in 2008—it wasn't healthy to continue to put pressure on his knee like this—but he wasn't going to get his knee attended to just yet.

Tiger started the 2008 season with an eight-stroke victory at the Buick Invitational, shooting an astonishing nineteen under par. The win marked his sixty-second PGA Tour victory, tying him with his idol, Arnold Palmer. It was his sixth victory at the event.

The following week, he was trailing by four strokes going into the final round of the Dubai Desert Classic, but he made six birdies on the back nine for a dramatic one-stroke victory. He took home his fifteenth World Golf Championship event at the Accenture Match Play Championship. He continued to grit his teeth through the pain, and few people knew about the torment his knee was causing him. All everyone else knew was that Tiger was back to dominating the tour, and that was a very good thing.

In March 2008, Tiger started slow in the Arnold Palmer Invitational, finishing the first round at even par; he was tied for thirty-fourth place. By the end of the third round, he was in a five-way tie for first place. He finished off the final two rounds with a pair of 66s, a strong enough showing to win his fifth consecutive PGA Tour victory with a dramatic twenty-four-foot putt on the eighteenth hole to defeat Bart Bryant by a stroke. It was his fifth career victory at this event, although at this point even Tiger would admit that statistics had become irrelevant.

But his streak was about to end. At the WGC-CA Championship, a tournament that Tiger had dominated for the previous three years, Gregg Ogilvy stopped Tiger's victorious run, beating him by two strokes. It was a minor loss and nothing that anyone got too worked up about.

Despite bold predictions that Tiger might again

challenge for the grand slam, he did not mount a serious charge at the 2008 Masters tournament, struggling with his putter through each round. He still finished alone in second, three strokes behind the champion, Trevor Immelman. His knee was killing him; he just couldn't focus as he used to, and he knew he needed to do something.

On April 15, 2008, Tiger announced that he needed knee surgery and would be stepping away from the tour for about two months. It wasn't the first indication anyone had that Tiger was experiencing knee pain; commentators knew that he had been flinching through his tournaments for the last ten months. He underwent his third surgery on his left knee in Park City, Utah. It was particularly painful, and he started taking Vicodin as a pain reliever.

While he was recuperating, the news surfaced that Tiger would be named *Men's Fitness* Fittest Athlete, again raising eyebrows about Tiger's cozy relationship with a second-tier fitness magazine. It wasn't a big deal, at least to most people, but golf magazines felt slighted to see their marquee star cooperating with a magazine outside the industry.

His knee healing, Tiger returned for the 2008 U.S. Open in one of the most anticipated golfing groupings in history. Tiger, Phil Mickelson, and Adam Scott were the top three golfers in the world, and they would play together. Tiger struggled in the first day on the course, notching a double bogey on his first hole. He ended the round at a one-over-par 72, four shots off the lead. On his second day, he scored a 68, three under par. Still paired with Phil, he managed five birdies, one eagle, and four bogeys. On the third day of the tournament, he once again started off with a double bogey and was trailing by five shots with six holes left to play. He finished the round by making two eagle putts, a combined one hundred feet in length, and a chip-in birdie to take a one-shot lead into the final round. His final putt assured that he would be in the final group for the sixth time in the last eight major championships.

On Sunday, June 15, Tiger began the day with yet another double bogey and trailed Rocco Mediate by one stroke. Tiger visibly winced after several of his tee shots and sometimes made an effort to keep weight off his left foot. He was behind by one stroke when he reached the final hole. Left with a twelve-foot putt for birdie, he made the shot to force an eighteen-hole playoff with Rocco on Monday.

Despite leading by as many as three strokes at one point in the playoff, Tiger again dropped back and needed to birdie the eighteenth to force sudden death with Rocco, which he did. Tiger made par on the first sudden death hole; Rocco subsequently missed his par putt, giving Tiger his fourteenth major championship.

His knee was still aching, and Tiger recognized

that the first surgery hadn't been sufficient to make the knee better. Tiger announced that he would be undergoing reconstructive surgery on his ACL. His season was over; he wouldn't compete until 2009. He would miss the Open Championship and the PGA Championship for the first time.

Tiger had sustained a double stress fracture in his left tibia while rehabbing after his April surgery. Publications throughout the world proclaimed his U.S. Open victory remarkable and lavished praise on his gutsy performance, especially after learning the extent of his knee injury. Tiger called it "my greatest ever championship —the best of the 14 because of all the things that have gone on over the past week."

During his time off, Tiger hired a new spokesman for his various business ventures. Glenn Greenspan had been the spokesman for Augusta National for several years. He knew golf, and he knew how to keep the media at bay. It wasn't uncommon for him to meet reporters at the gates of Augusta for an interview; he wouldn't let anyone on the property who didn't absolutely have to be there.

Glenn moved to Florida to become part of Tiger's inner circle. As part of his employment package, Glenn received a low-interest mortgage on a property in Stuart, Florida. The mortgage holder was one of Tiger's companies. Tiger believed in taking care of his employees; doing so made them more loyal.

There was an unexpected casualty of Tiger's injury shortened season: Television ratings for the PGA Tour dropped precipitously. Overall viewership for the second half of the 2008 season declined by 46.8 percent compared to 2007. Tiger was greatly missed; the sport needed him to recover quickly.

HE HAD BEEN GONE for only eight months, but Tiger's return to golf was billed as one of the most anticipated returns to sports in history. Golf was languishing without Tiger; ratings were down, and interest was sagging. Tiger's return was welcome news to everyone on the tour; all just hoped he would be in good enough condition to play convincingly and mount a charge for the top of the leaderboard.

Tiger's first PGA Tour event was at the World Golf Championship–Accenture Match Play Championship. A victory just wasn't in the cards, as he lost to Tim Clark in the second round. But Tiger was back; he had been profoundly missed.

Tiger won his first title of the year at the Arnold Palmer Invitational, where he was five strokes behind Sean O'Hair entering the final round. Tiger shot a final round 67 and made a sixteen-foot birdie putt at the final hole to defeat O'Hair by one stroke. It was a gratifying win before an exultant crowd, and the tour sponsors were ecstatic because the victory did as much for the sport of golf as for Tiger. He was back.

His return to golf wasn't quite as smooth as everyone had hoped; he wasn't dominating as he had been, but he was playing consistently, frequently challenging for the top spot, even if he ultimately came up short. At the 2009 Masters, he finished sixth, four strokes behind eventual winner Angel Cabrera. His performance wasn't a blowout, and there was no worry about another long-term slump; it would just take Tiger a little more time to get back into the sport. He'd soon be back to his dominating ways.

Tiger notched his second win of 2009 in June at the Memorial Tournament. After three rounds, he was trailing by four shots, and it appeared that he was going to continue his streak of almost winning, being nearly good enough. But he shot a final round of 65, including two consecutive birdies to end the tournament. It was another minor win—his fourth at this event—and no one attached too much significance to it. Everyone just liked seeing Tiger win again.

Tiger racked up four more wins in the season, again claiming the top spot on the list of PGA moneymakers. Despite his wins, Tiger endured one notable, rare failure: He had not made the cut at the U.S. Open, only the second time he hadn't made it to the top half of the leaderboard in a major throughout his entire career. For the first time since 2004, Tiger Woods had no major wins during the year.

TIGER HAD NEVER SPOKEN OUT about politics; it was one of the subjects that his publicity team members told reporters not to ask him about. Politics was personal, they said, and Tiger wanted to keep his views to himself. But Tiger's motives weren't solely about privacy, although that was part of his reticence. His team knew that political divisions could profoundly hurt his brand, and his managers didn't want to lose sales because people disagreed with Tiger's politics.

It would be easy to check Tiger's voter's registration, especially in Florida, where the information is included in several free databases. Tiger registered as an Independent, another way to keep his personal politics out of the public eye. Despite his seeming neutrality, he leaned Democratic on most issues. When Elin became a U.S. citizen, she registered as a Democrat. She had the luxury of choosing one of the political parties because she wasn't famous.

In 2009, Tiger finally decided to take a new step: He showed up at a political event to give a speech. Dressed in a dark suit, he braved the cold weather in Washington to make a short speech at Barack Obama's inauguration. In an introduction of the U.S. Naval Glee Club, Tiger invoked the memory of Earl:

I grew up in a military family—and my role models in life were my Mom and Dad, Lt. Colonel Earl Woods.

My dad was a Special Forces operator and many nights friends would visit our home. They represented every branch of service, and every rank. In my Dad, and in those guests, I saw first hand the dedication and commitment of those who serve. They come from every walk of life. From every part of our country. Time and again, across generations, they have defended our safety in the dark of night and far from home.

Each day—and particularly on this historic day—we honor the men and women in uniform who serve our country and protect our free-dom. They travel to the dangerous corners of the world, and we must remember that for every person who is in uniform, there are families who wait for them to come home safely.

I am honored that the military is such an important part, not just of my personal life, but of my professional life as well. The golf tournament we do each year here in Washington is a testament to those unsung heroes. I am the son of a man who dedicated his life to his country, family and the military, and I am a better person for it.

In the summer of 1864, Abraham Lincoln,

the man at whose memorial we stand, spoke to the 164th Ohio Regiment and said:

"I am greatly obliged to you, and to all who have come forward at the call of their country."

Just as they have stood tall for our country— we must always stand by and support the men and women in uniform and their families.

Thank you, and it is now my pleasure to introduce the U.S. Naval Glee Club.

Three months later, Tiger made his first White House visit, meeting with President Obama in the Oval Office. Standing side by side, Tiger and Obama looked strikingly similar as they posed for pictures together; they were arguably the two most famous black men in the world. Tiger's enthusiastic support of Obama had been enough to get the golfer to publicly identify, for the first time in his career, with a politician.

THE CROWD IN TIMES SQUARE pressed in on Tiger from all sides; there were easily a thousand people surrounding him, all attracted to him as if to a magnet. They called to him, begged for autographs, and snapped their cell phone cameras. Tiger, wearing his trademark red polo shirt and black pants, was struggling through the crowd, navigating like a salmon swimming upstream. Bodyguards tried to keep the swarming crowd away from Tiger, but they hadn't anticipated the number of people who would stop by for a glimpse of Tiger Woods.

It was a promotional day orchestrated by EA Sports as a way for Tiger to hype his latest video game, *Tiger Woods PGA Tour 10*. He had hooked up with comedian Jimmy Fallon to play a round of computerized golf on the big screens of Times Square. It was a lighthearted, fun event, showing off the video game to a large crowd.

By all appearances, Tiger was into the experience. He put on a great show, talking trash with Fallon and losing, badly, at his own game. Tour buses and taxis stopped in the middle of the road, their occupants gawking at the star. It was bedlam, an uncontrolled chaos that could be sparked only by an iconic, one-name star: Oprah, Madonna, Tiger.

When he got into a private area, he dropped the mask. Sipping from a bottle of water, Tiger sighed deeply, his shoulders drooping. At that moment, he looked, not like a young kid, but like a middle-aged man overwhelmed by the constant press of the crowd. It wasn't anything new to him; he had known these crowds for half of his life. But he was weary and tired.

"This is abnormal," he groused, half good-naturedly and half seriously. "This is so different from what my real life is. My real life is home with my family; this is just—I don't know, just crazy." The tone of his voice rose as he emphasized the word "crazy"; it was as if the public's attention still flabbergasted him, even though he had been a pro golfer for thirteen years.

Tiger was led to the Nike store where he would give a handful of interviews in front of a backdrop of Nike logos. It was a hectic media day, one that had started at dawn and would end with a corporate party, the worst kind, really, with small talk over shrimp puffs and miniature quiches. Tiger dutifully did what he was told, allowing his handlers to manhandle him, move him into position, and sit him down in front of the right reporters. Never before had Tiger seemed more a commodity, a prop in the play of his own career.

He had been making history on and off the course since his debut in 1996. By late 2009, thirteen years into his career, he had racked up seventy-one wins on the PGA Tour, including fourteen major titles, nine top prize money finishes, and nine Player of the Year awards. And he was only thirty-three.

Tiger's win at the FedEx Cup on September 27 earned him a $10 million bonus, which *Forbes* magazine reported pushed Tiger over the $1 billion threshold. Most of the money had come from endorsements; he was everywhere in both print ads and broadcast commercials, lending his name to sell everything from AT&T services to Nike shoes.

That money had bought Tiger a considerable

amount of the good life. His $2.4 million mansion in Windermere, Florida, was one of his least expensive properties. He had bought a $38 million twelve-acre waterfront compound on Jupiter Island, Florida, and had planned to move his family there. There was a $23 million home in Dubai, a $22 million 155-foot yacht, two multi-million dollar homes in California, and Elin's $2.3 million estate in Sweden. Tiger's career had been financially rewarding; he had enough money for many lifetimes.

Money was no longer Tiger's priority; he had all he could possibly ever need, and money became secondary to him. What Tiger had going for him was his reputation, his image as a golden boy. Not only did he have the money, but he also had the adoration of millions of fans.

CHAPTER 12

"ELIN, HOW DOES IT FEEL to be cheated on?" It was a rude question, one that would make any wife wince, but Elin stoically looked straight ahead, refusing to acknowledge the photographer who had tossed out the insensitive query. Wearing jeans, sunglasses, and a flannel shirt, she looked like any other pretty blonde woman in Orlando. The only difference was the mob scene in her wake.

She was just trying to pick her daughter up from school, not stop traffic near her Windermere home. The paparazzi lined up on the sidewalk: First there were only two, then there were five, and then there were fourteen, each of them running from a different direction as they aimed their cameras at Elin. She was the quarry, they were the hunters, and there was no way to escape; the school didn't have any hidden entrances. Flanked by a bodyguard, she opened the door and went into the school, knowing full well that she had to carry two-year-old Sam into the scrum.

As Elin exited the school building carrying Sam on her hip, the paparazzi called out to her, first pleading for her attention and then demanding it. A clear picture of Elin could sell for thousands of dollars; the stakes were high for the paparazzi, and they either didn't think or didn't care about the spectacle they were making. "Elin, over here," they continued to bark. "Elin, where's Tiger?" Sam stared at the phalanx of photographers with her wide eyes, then buried her face in her mother's shoulder.

"Get the fuck out of the way," a bodyguard bellowed at the circling photographers standing a few feet from Elin's SUV. "You guys are dirt. Do you hear me? Dirt!"

"We're just doing our job," a photographer yelled back at the bodyguard.

"Get a new job," the bodyguard replied. "Give her some space."

But space was the one luxury that Elin just couldn't buy, despite the millions of dollars at her disposal. The photographers continued to hoot at her as she went about her routine tasks: pumping gas, picking up Thai food, even going to the doctor. The only place that Elin had real privacy was inside the home that she had shared with Tiger, a beautiful mansion that now held so many bad memories.

She had briefly moved out to a rental home in the neighborhood; it was better than living at their eight-bedroom, nine-bathroom home where Tiger had allegedly carried on some of his affairs. But the children belonged in their own house; she wanted them to be surrounded by familiar things, so she moved everyone back home.

But she couldn't stay at home forever, and paparazzi stood outside the Isleworth gates ready to give chase. A quick trip to Starbucks would turn into a frenzy, and Elin often decided not to go out. It was just easier to be in a place where no one could take her picture.

While Elin faced crushing crowds, public scrutiny, and countless paparazzi photos of her and her children, Tiger vanished completely; there was no trace of the golfer, although the rumor mill worked overtime and speculation swirled wildly. News reports placed him everywhere from Dubai to New York, and many members of the public wondered how Tiger could just vanish, leaving Elin to face the music alone.

The pictures were published everywhere: in tabloids, in legitimate newspapers, even on cable news channels. Much was made over the fact that she wasn't wearing her wedding ring. Was this a deliberate gesture to send a message? Or was it a personal decision that reflected her feelings about her marriage? For that matter, had she worn her wedding ring throughout the marriage? No one knew, because no one had paid attention before now.

Elin Nordegren, for all her privacy and her eschewing of the limelight, was now one of the world's most sought after celebrities, famous by virtue of whom she had married. Her life as she knew it was gone; even if she remained married to Tiger, she would always be partially in the public eye. People who didn't know what she looked like now saw her splashed across the news; she could never anonymously go about her business again.

SCANDALS HAVE THE POWER to instantly erase years of good works, and Tiger's fall from grace was particularly steep. Tiger Woods was no longer known as a golden boy who had transformed a sport while raising two children with his devoted wife. He was now labeled as the world's most famous sex addict, a man whose proclivities were so extensive that very few of his fans were able to absolve him of guilt. Everything took a hit in the aftermath of the scandal. Donations to the Tiger Woods Foundation dropped precipitously; sales of his merchandise sagged; people didn't want to have his famous "TW" logo on their clothes. His image was in ruins, and no one was around to pick up the pieces.

Throughout the 2009 holiday season, Tiger Woods never came out of hiding; he was not seen or photographed anywhere, and his absence perpetuated the scandal more than his presence might have. He was missing, and the mystery propelled the story forward in the media. Tiger was fodder not only for the tabloids, but also for legitimate press covering the scandal; news of his affairs splashed across ESPN. The prevalence of the Tiger Woods story, combined with his vanishing act, gave the story some added intrigue. Had he made an appearance—just an innocuous sighting of him anywhere—the rumors might not have gotten as frenzied as they did. But having unlimited funds can give a man the wherewithal to vanish completely, and Tiger became a reclusive ghost who faded out of sight, if not out of mind.

Tiger Woods, the man who had become the darling of corporate America, was now a pariah. Companies didn't want endorsements by mere mortals; they wanted a god, and Tiger had been a deity for more than a decade. With the realization that he had foibles, his attractiveness to sponsors was tarnished.

Accenture, the management consultancy firm that had partnered with Tiger since 2003, was the first to drop Tiger. In December, the firm issued a straightforward and unsentimental statement: "For the past six years, Accenture and Tiger Woods have had a very successful sponsorship and his achievements on the golf course have been a powerful metaphor for business success in Accenture's advertising. However, given the circumstances of the last two weeks, after careful consideration and analysis, the company has determined that he is no longer the right representative for its advertising. Accenture wishes only the best for Tiger Woods and his family."

It was the first domino to fall; others followed. Gillette soon announced that it would temporarily halt its advertising with Tiger, so that he could get his head straight and work out the personal issues he faced: "In the midst of a difficult and unfortunate situation, we respect the action Tiger is taking to restore the trust of his family, friends and fans. We fully support him stepping back from his professional career and taking the time he needs to do what matters most. We wish him and his family the best. As Tiger takes a break from the public eye, we will support his desire for privacy by limiting his role in our marketing programs."

It was a nicely worded release, which seemed to show genuine concern for Tiger and his family. Still, there was no denying that the statement was the easiest way to dispatch controversy; Tiger was a damaged brand, and Gillette had found a compassionate and gentle way to step away from him.

But the devastating blows continued, and AT&T, once Tiger's second-largest corporate endorsement deal, also decided to back away from him. "We are ending our sponsorship agreement with Tiger Woods and wish him well in the future," the company said in its statement.

Nike, the first and most lucrative endorsement deal that Tiger had ever received, vowed to stand behind him, although the company immediately removed his ads from television. It was the equivalent of a man embarrassed to be seen with his wife who had lost her looks: sure, they'd stay married, but they wouldn't make any public appearances together. Over the years, Nike had paid Tiger more than $110 million. To walk away now would be devastating to Nike; it would be left without a marquee star.

The decision was even more difficult at EA Sports, the video game company that had released a new Tiger Woods game every year. For fourteen months prior to the scandal, EA had spent nearly $40 million on an online game based on Tiger's golf swing. Stepping away from Tiger, at least at this point, would cost EA Sports considerable time and money. After weeks of internal discussions, the company decided to go forward with the game. Peter Moore, the president of EA Sports, released a statement to the media:

> For the past month, we have watched the Tiger Woods story play itself out while several of his sponsors have stepped away from the golfer. At EA Sports, we've been particularly attentive because for the past year, we have been in full development of a new and highly innovative online golf game. . . . We have spent considerable time developing and testing this game, we are proud of it, and we are releasing it in open beta later this month.
>
> This decision will no doubt create some attention and further speculation about Tiger Woods and about his relationship with sponsors. With that in mind, I want to shed some light on why EA Sports has decided to continue with Tiger on the masthead of this game.

Our relationship with Tiger has always been rooted in golf. We didn't form a relationship with him so that he could act as an arm's length endorser. Far from it. We chose to partner with Tiger in 1997 because we saw him as the world's best, most talented and exciting golfer. We struck that partnership with the assumption that he would remain near or at the top of his sport for years to come.

By his own admission, he's made some mistakes off the course. But regardless of what's happening in his personal life, and regardless of his decision to take a personal leave from the sport, Tiger Woods is still one of the greatest athletes in history.

The pattern was now clear: Companies that were directly tied to the golf industry were standing by Tiger, whereas companies that used Tiger as part of a broader brand-building initiative were cutting their ties with him and developing new marketing strategies.

The freefall of Tiger Woods's personal life was mirrored by his career nosedive. Now he wasn't playing golf; he was on an "indefinite" leave. A study by the University of California, Davis determined that the companies that Tiger endorsed had collectively lost $12 billion in stock value in the month after the scandal broke. He had once helped these companies increase their earnings and raise their profiles. He had been their Superman; now he was their kryptonite.

AFTER THE SONY OPEN on January 12, Jesper Parnevik spoke to reporters about the scandal, his first public comments since he had publicly blasted Tiger a month earlier. Asked if he regretted calling Tiger out for his indiscretions, Jesper replied, "If I would have said something politically correct, I don't think I could have looked Elin in the eye."

Jesper also admitted what everyone around Tiger had been saying: that the rumors of his infidelity had long been swirling around the golfing community—rumors that Jesper would then vocally refute. "More and more, you hear guys say, 'We knew about it,'" Jesper told reporters. "I had no idea. Actually, I heard people sometimes say, 'We heard that Tiger had two blondes around his arm,' and I would say, 'No way, that was Elin and her sister.' Every story, I said, 'That can't be right. Tiger would never do anything like that.' It was a big shock to me."

The shock had worn off, and golfers started speaking to the media about Tiger's problems. Sure, they wanted him back on the tour; he was the reason that the ratings were so high and consequently that everyone was making so much money. Tiger wasn't simply a moneymaker for himself; his Midas touch extended to everyone on the tour, and tour members needed him.

But needing him and liking him were two different things. Tiger might raise the PGA profile, but he was drawing the wrong type of attention to golf. Tiger had been on the cover of the *New York Post* for twenty-one consecutive days in December—one more than the newspaper had covered the September 11 terrorist attacks. Tiger had gone from being an athlete to a tabloid fixture. Even when he came back, things would be markedly different.

"WORLD EXCLUSIVE PHOTOS: First pictures of Tiger Woods in Sex Rehab." The headline on the Web site was huge, with orange and red letters that screamed what everyone had been speculating. The *National Enquirer* had published grainy photos, taken with a telephoto lens, on its Web site, RadarOnline.com.

The pictures themselves were nothing exciting: a thin black man wearing a baseball cap and a hooded sweatshirt, all but unidentifiable. It certainly could have been Tiger Woods, or it could have been any number of other black men with the same build. The picture itself was inconclusive.

The accompanying article claimed that Tiger had checked into Pine Grove Behavioral Health and Addiction Services. He was alleged to have entered into Gentle Path, a sex addiction recovery program that treated sexually compulsive behavior. The article was explicit in the details: no sex, masturbation, or pornography. Patients were required to confess their sexual sins to their significant others, giving details and specifics as a way to reestablish trust. It seemed an unlikely place for Tiger to turn up. Pine Grove was not the typical celebrity rehab center. The amenities were modest, and the center was in a rundown section of Hattiesburg, Mississippi. Flanked by KFCs and check-cashing stores, Pine Grove certainly seemed like no place for a superstar athlete.

The day after the story hit the Web, the administration of Pine Grove hired a carpenter to build a tall fence, a way to protect patients. In reality, the fence was little more than large black tarps nailed to plywood and two-by-fours. The tarps looked like garbage bags, making the entire fence an eyesore, but neighbors around the center weren't the type who had the high ground to complain about eyesores.

The following day, a Tiger lookalike purposefully strode around the grounds in plain view, clearly hoping to be photographed. The paparazzi happily snapped pictures of this new man, convinced that the *Enquirer* had mistaken this man for Tiger Woods. The *Enquirer* insisted that the lookalike was an imposter, intended to throw the media off Tiger's trail.

The truth is that the *Enquirer* was at least partially right: Tiger was at the clinic, but not living on the grounds. Instead, he stayed in a private cabin as he worked through his issues and demons. Elin flew up at least twice, spending time with Tiger and attending intense therapy with him. She stopped by a few local stores and restaurants, her hair pulled back, her eyes puffy. She had seemed so strong in Orlando, but now it looked as if the stress was tearing her apart. He stayed for six weeks before flying home to Orlando, where he and Elin both stayed in the family home. Whether or not she decided to stay with him, and whether or not the therapy had been successful, they had a long road ahead of them.

According to several sources at Pine Grove, one of the necessary components of the program was apology. Patients suffering from sex addiction were required to apologize to everyone who had been harmed through their behavior. This requirement would present a difficult dilemma for Tiger, who lived such a public life. Millions of people had been hurt or disillusioned by his behavior. How could he possibly apologize to them all?

CHAPTER 13

TIGER WOODS HAD BEEN A HUGE STAR before his car accident, but the scandal made him an even bigger celebrity. News editors and televison program directors thought that he had never been so interesting, and the public didn't seem to tire of the wall-to-wall coverage of the scandal. People speculated about when Tiger would reappear and in what venue. In mid-February 2010, they got their answer.

The announcement first appeared on Tiger's Web site and was then quickly disseminated around the country to hundreds of newsrooms and studios: Tiger Woods would address the scandal publicly for the first time at 11 a.m. on Friday, February 19, at the PGA headquarters in Ponte Vedra Beach, Florida. The ground rules were simple: Only a select few reporters and photographers would be allowed in the room. One camera would serve as a pool camera. Tiger would read from a prepared statement, and there would be no questions.

The timing of the speech proved to be controversial. Tiger's statement would happen in the middle of the WGC-Accenture Match Play Championship. Many golfers felt that it was typical Tiger: doing whatever he wanted to do with little regard for other players. Ernie Els, a golfer whom Tiger had always considered a friend, issued a blunt quote about the timing. "It's selfish," he told *Golfweek* magazine. "You can write that. I feel sorry for the sponsor. Mondays are a good day to make statements, not Friday. This takes a lot away from the golf tournament."

Ernie had never spoken so harshly about Tiger before, and the two golfers had never had problems in the past. Several golf publications postulated that Ernie's candid statements were indicative of the sentiment among PGA players.

Ernie was the first to speak out, but he was not the last. Rory McIlroy suggested to *Golf Digest* that Tiger had planned the statement in the middle of Accenture's tournament as a way to get back at the sponsor that had been the first one to drop him.

Golfer Jay Williamson took to his Twitter account to sound off against Tiger. "Hopefully, fans see through the farce of Friday's party in Florida," he wrote. Later in the week, he tweeted again. "Character flaw of mine," he wrote, "but not much sympathy for a billionaire with a sex addiction—maybe more like pity." In subsequent interviews, Williamson said he was just saying what he was hearing on the driving range and in the locker room.

In fact, several golfers had gone on record to criticize Tiger. Legendary golfer Tom Watson had spoken about Tiger in an interview with KSHB, the NBC affiliate in Kansas City. "His golf is really secondary at this point," Watson said.

"From his standpoint and his family's standpoint, it's something he needs to get control of, and make some amends and show some humility to the public when he comes back."

Watson continued pointedly, taking aim at Tiger's etiquette on the golf course. "His swearing and his club throwing, that should end," he said definitively. "That's not part of what we want to project as far as the professional golf tour is concerned." He then went on to say that Tiger's actions were "bad for the game."

Tiger had received some encouragement from one golfer. "It's important for him to come back and be part of the sport," Phil Mickelson told reporters. "But right now, he's got a lot more important things going on in his life. [My wife] Amy and I are good friends with both Tiger and Elin, and we care deeply about how this turns out. But I'm going to choose not to talk about it publicly anymore, and I appreciate your understanding on that."

Clearly, Tiger had a long way to go to make amends to many of his fellow golfers, most of whom were wondering when he'd come back to the tour. Whether the golfers liked Tiger or not, their futures were dependent upon his decision. Tiger's speech would have to address them as well.

AFTER THREE MONTHS OUT of the public eye, Tiger was easing back into view. The Wednesday before his speech, the first series of photographs of Tiger in three months emerged. They were innocuous pictures: Tiger jogging along the streets of Isleworth near his home. He looked a little bit heavier, at least in the pictures, and he was decked out in Nike clothing from head to toe. He was accompanied by his regular workout partner, twenty-three-year-old Corey Carroll. Tiger was not wearing his wedding ring.

Members of the media were immediately suspicious of the circumstances surrounding the shots. They were too clear to be paparazzi photos. They had been taken at just the right time of day for ideal lighting. The expressions on his face were too perfect. And reporters knew that there was no way that a paparazzo would have been able to get into the gates of Isleworth to take a candid shot. Everything about the photos seemed to be a publicity stunt.

Sam Greenwood, a longtime PGA photographer and contributor to *Sports Illustrated,* had taken several pictures that day, many of which were distributed through Getty Images. Getty was charging a nominal fee for the pictures' distribution, thus neutralizing the incentive for paparazzi photographers to get the first picture of a postscandal Tiger. Getty gave no indication that the photos were staged. They were immediately circulated in the media, even though most reporters doubted that the pictures were little more than promotional shots.

Come to find out, the photos had been meticulously planned and controlled. The next day—less than twenty-four hours before Tiger was to make his statement—more photos emerged. This set of photos showed a Nike-clad Tiger swinging a golf club on his home course of Isleworth, just yards from his back door. He was smiling, looking carefree—and not wearing his wedding band. But these pictures looked poised, even though they were sold as news photos. Paparazzi agency Splash News had shot pictures of the photo shoot, clearly showing that Greenwood and Tiger were setting up the shots together. It seemed that Tiger would continue to manage his media, not leaving anything to chance. Indeed, he seemed to have become even more controlling of his media.

NOT SINCE OJ SIMPSON'S infamous Bronco chase in 1994 had the nation been so riveted by such a public and widely broadcast spectacle. People across the country huddled in front of televisions in airports, gyms, and restaurants to hear what he had to say. Hundreds of people stopped in Times Square to watch Tiger's face on the large television screens. Activity nearly screeched to a halt at the New York Stock Exchange as traders stopped to watch Tiger apologize. The Winter Olympics were preempted. For the thirteen minutes that Tiger spoke, people around the world stopped and stared at their television screens. This was his biggest audience ever. His average golf tournament drew nearly 5 million viewers, but his speech drew nearly 30 million people, many of whom were not even golf fans. Twenty-two broadcast and cable networks broke into programming to air Tiger's comments live. An additional 12 million listened to the speech on the radio. And Web traffic was so heavy on ESPN.com that the site slowed down significantly. Tiger's apology was no longer just a news story; it was now an event.

The hoopla surrounding the speech almost over-shadowed the fact that the speech was a moment of personal reckoning for Tiger. He hadn't slept well the night before; he told friends that he had woken up several times during the night as he thought about the message he was about to give. He awoke before dawn and practiced his speech once again. His public persona was dependent on what he was about to say, and although his reps told the world that this was a public statement of private remorse, they recognized that it was more important than that: The future of Tiger's brand hung in the balance.

Shortly after 11:00 a.m., Tiger entered the room where he would start rehabilitating his image. Forty people, including friends, business associates, PGA Tour executives, and Tiger's team members, sat in three rows of wooden chairs set in an arc, waiting for him to arrive. Kultida Woods sat in the front row, just off to Tiger's right, looking straight ahead with a somber expression on her face. The three windows in the small room were shut tightly, their blinds drawn. Heavy blue drapes at the front of the room opened, and Tiger Woods emerged publicly for the first time in more than three months.

More than a mile away, nearly 450 members of the press sat in a ballroom of a Marriott Hotel, watching the events unfold on six big-screen television sets. Before Tiger appeared, many people chattered and laughed raucously, as if they were at a Superbowl party rather than a news event. When he emerged, the assembled reporters and photographers instantly became quiet, ready to document every word that Tiger said.

Analysts would later disagree about Tiger's delivery of the speech. Some would say it was robotic and insincere. Others would say he was candid and open. The truth was probably somewhere in between. He had clearly rehearsed the speech—perhaps too many times to sound genuine —but he delivered it well, with a strong voice that occasionally shook as he addressed the nation.

Tiger stood in front of the podium and sighed visibly before starting his speech. "Good morning, and thank you for joining me," he began purposefully as the cameras flashed. "Many of you in this room are my friends. Many of you in this room know me. Many of you have cheered for me or you've worked with me or you've supported me.

"Now every one of you has good reason to be critical of me. I want to say to each of you, simply and directly, I am deeply sorry for the irresponsible and selfish behavior I engaged in. I know people want to find out how I could be so selfish and so foolish. People want to know how I could have done these things to my wife, Elin, and to my children. And while I have always tried to be a private person, there are some things I want to say."

As Tiger paused, Kultida dabbed her eyes. She appeared to blink back tears as she fixed her gaze on her son as he did one of the hardest things of his life. Tiger looked down at his notes and continued to speak.

"Elin and I have started the process of discussing the damage caused by my behavior. As Elin pointed out to me, my real apology to her will not come in the form of words; it will come from my behavior over time. We have a lot to discuss; however, what we say to each other will remain between the two of us.

"I am also aware of the pain my behavior has caused to those of you in this room," he continued. "I have let you down, and I have let down my fans. For many of you, especially my friends, my behavior has been a personal disappointment. To those of you who work for me, I have let you down personally and professionally. My behavior has caused considerable worry to my business partners.

"To everyone involved in my foundation,

including my staff, board of directors, sponsors, and most importantly, the young students we reach, our work is more important than ever. Thirteen years ago, my dad and I envisioned helping young people achieve their dreams through education. This work remains unchanged and will continue to grow. From the Learning Center students in Southern California to the Earl Woods scholars in Washington, D.C., millions of kids have changed their lives, and I am dedicated to making sure that continues."

In the media room, a low murmur buzzed among the assembled reporters, many of whom were surprised that he would give what appeared to be a plug for his charity in the midst of his statement. He pressed on, referring to his notes again.

"But still, I know I have bitterly disappointed all of you. I have made you question who I am and how I could have done the things I did. I am embarrassed that I have put you in this position." He paused for a moment, appearing to choke up. "For all that I have done, I am so sorry.

"I have a lot to atone for," he sighed before slightly raising his voice defiantly, "but there is one issue I really want to discuss. Some people have speculated that Elin somehow hurt or attacked me on Thanksgiving night. It angers me that people would fabricate a story like that. Elin never hit me that night or any other night. There has never been an episode of domestic violence in our marriage, ever. Elin has shown enormous grace and poise throughout this ordeal. Elin deserves praise, not blame. The issue involved here was my repeated irresponsible behavior. I was unfaithful. I had affairs. I cheated. What I did is not acceptable, and I am the only person to blame."

He continued, "I stopped living by the core values that I was taught to believe in. I knew my actions were wrong, but I convinced myself that normal rules didn't apply. I never thought about who I was hurting. Instead, I thought only about myself. I ran straight through the boundaries that a married couple should live by. I thought I could get away with whatever I wanted to. I felt that I had worked hard my entire life and deserved to enjoy all the temptations around me. I felt I was entitled. Thanks to money and fame, I didn't have to go far to find them. I was wrong. I was foolish. I don't get to play by different rules. The same boundaries that apply to everyone apply to me. I brought this shame on myself. I hurt my wife, my kids, my mother, my wife's family, my friends, my foundation, and kids all around the world who admired me."

In the front row, Kultida looked down at her hands folded in her lap. Next to her sat Amy Reynolds, a Nike executive who had been crying throughout the entire speech. Kultida looked back up at her son as he continued.

"I've had a lot of time to think about what I've

done. My failures have made me look at myself in a way I never wanted to before. It's now up to me to make amends, and that starts by never repeating the mistakes I've made. It's up to me to start living a life of integrity.

"I once heard, and I believe it's true, it's not what you achieve in life that matters; it's what you overcome. Achievements on the golf course are only part of setting an example. Character and decency are what really count. Parents used to point to me as a role model for their kids. I owe all those families a special apology. I want to say to them that I am truly sorry.

"It's hard to admit that I need help, but I do," he continued. "For forty-five days from the end of December to early February, I was in inpatient therapy receiving guidance for the issues I'm facing. I have a long way to go. But I've taken my first steps in the right direction."

A noticeable buzz reverberated through the press room. Many of the reporters had predicted that Tiger would never get specific about his problems and his treatment, and his admission that he was going through treatment was unexpected. The reporters typed furiously on their laptops.

"As I proceed, I understand people have questions," he said evenly. "I understand the press wants to ask me for the details and the times I was unfaithful. I understand people want to know whether Elin and I will remain together. Please know that as far as I'm concerned, every one of these questions and answers is a matter between Elin and me." His voice became more forceful. "These are issues between a husband and a wife.

"Some people have made up things that never happened. They said I used performance-enhancing drugs. This is completely and utterly false. Some have written things about my family. Despite the damage I have done, I still believe it is right to shield my family from the public spotlight. They did not do these things; I did.

"I have always tried to maintain a private space for my wife and children. They have been kept separate from my sponsors, my commercial endorsements. When my children were born, we only released photographs so that the paparazzi could not chase them." He became forceful and intense as he continued. "However, my behavior doesn't make it right for the media to follow my two-and-a-half-year-old daughter to school and report the school's location. They staked out my wife and they pursued my mom. Whatever my wrong-doings, for the sake of my family, please leave my wife and kids alone.

"I recognize I have brought this on myself, and I know above all I am the one who needs to change. I owe it to my family to become a better person. I owe it to those closest to me to become a better man. That's where my focus will be. I have a lot of work to do, and I intend to dedicate myself to doing it.

"Part of following this path for me is Buddhism, which my mother taught me at a young age. People probably don't realize it, but I was raised a Buddhist, and I actively practiced my faith from childhood until I drifted away from it in recent years. Buddhism teaches that a craving for things outside ourselves causes an unhappy and pointless search for security. It teaches me to stop following every impulse and to learn restraint. Obviously I lost track of what I was taught."

He cleared his throat. "As I move forward, I will continue to receive help because I've learned that's how people really do change. Starting tomorrow, I will leave for more treatment and more therapy. I would like to thank my friends at Accenture and the players in the field this week for understanding why I'm making these remarks today."

Kultida continued to sit motionless as she watched Tiger, her hands still folded in her lap. She blinked several times, as if to hold back tears.

"In therapy, I've learned the importance of looking at my spiritual life and keeping in balance with my professional life. I need to regain my balance and be centered so I can save the things that are most important to me, my marriage and my children. That also means relying on others for help. I've learned to seek support from my peers in therapy, and I hope someday to return that support to others who are seeking help.

"I do plan to return to golf one day," he said. "I just don't know when that day will be. I don't rule out that it will be this year. When I do return, I need to make my behavior more respectful of the game. In recent weeks I have received many thousands of emails, letters and phone calls from people expressing good wishes.

"To everyone who has reached out to me and my family, thank you. Your encouragement means the world to Elin and me. I want to thank the PGA Tour, Commissioner Finchem, and the players for their patience and understanding while I work on my private life. I look forward to seeing my fellow players on the course.

"Finally, there are many people in this room, and there are many people at home who believed in me," Tiger said, before looking directly into the camera for maximum effect. "Today I want to ask for your help. I ask you to find room in your heart to one day believe in me again."

EPILOGUE

FROM THE MOMENT that two-year-old Tiger Woods appeared on *Mike Douglas,* he was becoming a brand, a magnetic persona that would earn him more than $1 billion. Each win, each endorsement, each interview was a carefully selected brick that formed a wall around Tiger, insulating him from the harsh realities of the outside world. Tiger Woods had created a fortress of privilege for himself. For years, everyone thought it was impenetrable. Tiger Woods was one of the world's most untouchable stars, seemingly above scandal.

He meticulously polished his image, making only the shrewdest moves, keeping himself away from the media. Although many people thought he was eschewing the media to hide his sexual indiscretions, the truth was far more pedestrian. He just didn't want anyone to get too close, to break his or her way into Tiger's inner circle. The only people he allowed into his life, besides his family and his managers, were the very women who would bring him down.

Tiger had always spoken highly of Elin; she was a strong woman, he said, much more intelligent than people gave her credit for being. After the scandal, many wondered how she could possibly stay with him; he had broken her trust so many times. Why didn't she just leave? But the decision was hers, the reasons were between her and Tiger, and whether or not they ultimately stayed together would be worked out in private, not in the pages of the tabloids.

Whether or not Elin and Tiger stayed together would be a private matter, but his future in golf would not be. He had chosen a public lifestyle, and regardless of his protests of privacy, it was the publicity that had helped him become a billionaire. Tiger Woods had sold his privacy for ten figures, and everyone had an opinion about him, both before and after the scandal.

The Tiger Woods whom the world knew before November 2009 is gone forever; in fact his private life may never have matched his public persona. But despite a ruined reputation, desertion by his sponsors, plummeting popularity, and a general anger toward him, Tiger still has one very compelling ace in the hole: He is still one of the best golfers—if not *the* best golfer—to ever play the game. That will probably not ever be enough to fully restore his public image as perhaps the most beloved athlete in the world, but he can rest knowing that he might be the most talented in his chosen sport. In December 2009, in the midst of the scandal, the Associated Press named Tiger the Athlete of the Decade, proving that his athletic prowess will always be rewarded, regardless of Tiger's personal failings.

The scandal will forever trail Tiger's name; it will run in his obituary and will be a part of every news article written about him. But Tiger's resilience has always been his strength; even though he won't bounce back completely, the world will see a new Tiger Woods, one with foibles and flaws. Tiger Woods will no longer be considered an untouchable god; he has now proved that he is only human.

ACKNOWLEDGMENTS

I WISH TO THANK the following corporations and institutions for their outstanding assistance and support: the PGA, *Golf* magazine, the Golf Channel, *Links* magazine, the Florida Highway Patrol, the Windermere Police Department, the Ninth Judicial Circuit Court of Florida, Kansas State University, Cerritos Elementary School, Western High School, and Stanford University.

Although many friends and associates of Tiger Woods were willing to provide information for the book, they were also reluctant to be quoted for attribution. I am grateful for their insightful contributions and have respected their request for anonymity. I am grateful to Tom Cunneff, Connell Barrett, Irene Folstrom, and Tammy Reeder for their guidance.

I also wish to thank my colleagues at *People* magazine, many of whom pointed me in the right direction in researching this book. Special thanks to Amy Green, Wendy Grossman, Kristen Harmel, Kristen Mascia, Liz McNeil, Kathy Ehrich Dowd, and Michelle Tauber.

I am also grateful to my editor, Kevin Hanover, and the rest of the team at Da Capo Press.

Without their commitment and vision, this book would not be possible. I also want to thank Christine Marra at *Marra*thon Editorial Production Services for her valuable input.

Above all, I wish to thank my agent, Maura Teitelbaum, for her support and guidance.